THE MAN FROM ZARA

THE MAN FROM ZARA

THE STORY OF THE GENIUS BEHIND THE INDITEX GROUP

Covadonga O'Shea

LONDON   NEW YORK
MADRID   BARCELONA
MEXICO CITY   MONTERREY
BOGOTÁ   BUENOS AIRES

Published by
LID Publishing Ltd.
6-8 Underwood Street
London N1 7JQ (United Kingdom)
Ph. +44 (0)20 7831 8883
info@lidpublishing.com
LIDPUBLISHING.COM

A member of B P R

www.businesspublishersroundtable.com

© La Esfera de los Libros, S.L., 2008.
  Original title: *Así es Amancio Ortega, el hombre que creo Zara*
© Covadonga O'Shea, 2008
© LID Publishing Ltd. 2012

Printed in Great Britain by T J International Ltd.

ISBN: 978-1-907794-20-9
Collection editor: Jeanne Bracken
Translation: Don Topley
Editing: Laurie Price
Cover design: Irene Lorenzo
Typesetting: SyS Alberquilla S.L.

First edition: March 2012

Contents

Contents

Foreword

Covadonga O'Shea walked into my office in the School of Fashion at Parsons in New York exuding style and fierce intelligence. Chic, elegant and sophisticated it was immediately clear this was a woman Parsons wanted to work with. Since then, we have met many times including when she invited me to speak at ISEM the MBA school that she leads in Madrid. On each occasion my respect for her and her perspective on this glorious global fashion industry has grown. So it is only natural that the hitherto closed world of Zara has been opened up for her to chronicle.

Many years earlier, when I worked as a fashion designer in London, an important stop on our Parisian research trips was always the Zara store near L'Opera in Paris. We needed to see how Zara had interpreted key trends. We were used to seeing the full season's offers from other stores, but somehow Zara always surprised us. Colleagues visiting the store a couple of weeks later would see completely different stock. We marvelled at how quickly the store changed.

Many people question the quick turn around of a new season's colours or silhouettes or hem-lines. But without the transient nature of fashion trends, garment inspectors in India, shop assistants in England, tech designers in the USA, window dressers in Spain, knitters in Thailand, sewing machinists in Mexico and tens of millions of others in fashion related jobs around the world would not be working.

Of course fashion is also a lot of fun. For a consumer choosing a fabulous new party dress, to a designer creating a striking new look, there is a basic social need being fulfilled, the need to look and feel good.

In this book, Covadonga O'Shea delves into the origins of Zara, how the company evolved into the global fashion player we know today and crucially how it still manages to react so quickly to trends around the world. And while there is a necessary debate about the sustainability of fast fashion, there is also the fact that thanks to companies like Zara, millions of people who cannot afford couture can still look and feel good.

There is much to learn from Zara's story and Covadonga O'Shea brings a highly informed and intelligent perspective to it.

Simon Collins
Dean. School of Fashion
Parsons the New School for Design
New York City

Acknowledgements

I am indebted to a large number of people for their help with the publication of this book.

First and foremost, of course, is the protagonist, Amancio Ortega himself, who, over a period of a number of years, little by little revealed hidden corners of his personality and his work which, despite his resistance, opened the door to his permission to set down what he tells in these pages.

He is then followed by a long list of people who work or who have worked at Inditex, whose opinions and stories have helped me portray the man and his company with the greatest possible precision. My warmest gratitude to each and every one of them. It would be impossible here to include every single name, but let me assure you all that not a single name has been forgotten.

And my thanks, yet again, go to secretaries Raquel, Maribel and Carmen who, with their endless patience and efforts, far exceeding the call of duty, have been invaluable allies.

And many thanks to the current President of Inditex, Pablo Isla, who provided me with the utmost support to help me succeed in allowing the world to know something of the person who is Amancio Ortega, the founder of this organisation. He never failed to urge me to keep going and he spent a great deal of time reading through this document so that I should enjoy peace of mind in the knowledge that everything was in order.

And last but not least, I thank LID Publishing for bringing this keenly awaited and much needed version in English to the market.

Madrid, November 2011

Introduction

It never occurred to me to write this book until suddenly, one day I realised that not only did I want to write it, but that I was under a compulsion to sit down at the computer and set about telling the world into which Amancio Ortega's business has exploded so spectacularly. This is everything I have been lucky enough to learn about this man through my meetings with him. He is just a man, yet he became so much more because of his absolute candour. Because of Amancio Ortega's passion for anonymity he has defended his privacy against attempts by others to destroy it. He has completely and unintentionally become an almost mythical figure in the world of business, yet he has undoubtedly made history in spite of his desire to remain anonymous.

Endless tales have been told about him, none with any foundation, and his true personality is still unknown. The business schools that head up the international rankings of those aspiring to be experts examine his career and all of those who have spoken to him even just one time act as though he were an old acquaintance. The most they can really boast about is that they might have shaken hands with him once.

You will not find me making any absurd claims here, such as that I am one of Amancio's close circle of friends or colleagues who he deals with on a daily basis; but I do consider myself rather privileged because since the outset of our relationship we have spent quite a lot of time in contact. I have been able to talk with him about almost anything at all, just as an exchange of views between two professionals who happen to be passionate about their work. He was already a groundbreaker in his field, en route to achieve the greatest business success in the 20th century in the field of fashion. My own field, fronting the magazine *Telva*, a pioneer in the world of women's national publications, could also make claims to having conquered a market that was beginning to fill up with competitors keen to control the national product.

Were we united by a common vision of the future and an almost blind faith in what was in our hands? Leaving aside all our differences, I do not have the slightest doubt that something along those lines must have taken place for that initial trust, now over a quarter of a century old, to have persisted over the years and not lose an iota of its closeness and brilliance.

I met Amancio Ortega on December the first 1990, when I was invited to visit Inditex (Industries in Design in Textiles), a large textile business located in the outskirts of La Coruña, a province in northwest Spain. At that time the name of the small industrial zone way up there in Finisterre, Arteixo (the outskirts of La Coruña), was hardly known at all. These days it is talked about on five continents. When I landed, as has been the case every time I visited, a car was waiting for me in the airport. I was then taken to what was Zara's general headquarters at the time, near the magnificent building that was built years later in the same Sabón zone. I came to chat with the founder of a textile business that was just beginning to attract a great deal of attention, and I was taking the opportunity to have a look at the plant.

I never anticipated that the meeting would become the starting point of what I decided to do: communicate what lies behind those four letters, Zara, the flagship of an extraordinary company, Inditex. The company heads a world-wide retail business and is ranked number one among Spanish companies according to the Merco 2008 report (business monitor of corporate ranking). This is a business model that revolutionised the complex and exciting world of fashion. Because of the tireless labours of Amancio Ortega and the hundreds of individuals at his side over the years, a huge leap forward from the 20th into the 21st century was taken in the women's clothing sector.

On many occasions, listening to Amancio or the people around him, I personally witnessed the way this business works, the engine that lies behind those mega-figures that we read about in the media, how he won his personal fortune, the millions and millions of kilometres of raw materials used to supply products to the thousands of shops of different brands spread out throughout the world in record time, how his employees and their families live, and so much more.

I assure you that regardless of the friendship that Amancio and I share, and the many hours of conversation we have enjoyed, he never gave me the slightest reason to think that I might receive his permission to write this book. This means that any attempt on my part to do so would be like a betrayal or a breach of his right to privacy. My efforts, verging on pig-headedness, to reveal the more personal and human side of this man were witnessed by his closest colleagues: the remarkable José María Castellano (former CEO and deputy chairman of the Inditex Group), essential to the whole story and its understanding, and his magnificent successor, Pablo Isla (current chairman and CEO of Inditex since July 2011.) They both heard me talk about the many occasions on which I suggested my idea to Amancio, "You have to realise that it would simply be unfair not to explain to the world what kind of man you are. You have to accept that the fact of being at the high end on the list of the richest men in Spain and, indeed, one of the richest in the world, doesn't explain anything fundamental about you. Yes, it says you made a fortune, but paradoxical as it may seem, it provides a very poor picture of what you're like as a human being. It's much more important for you to explain your points of view, the things that are key. Who is Amancio Ortega really? Where did he come from? Where is he headed? What started him off dreaming about this empire that is now a visible and measurable reality?"

I never let myself be put off by his remorseless refusals. I felt sure that one day the conviction and strength of my argument would win him over and he would realise that I was right. Indeed what happened, after a good many years, was that while he didn't actually say I had his complete support for the project, which would have amounted to him rejecting his most deeply held principles, he sent a message that was the sweetest gift, "You must do what you want – after all, I can't actually stop you from writing. I trust you." He suggested, "And don't just put in the good parts, or say that it was me alone who built the firm. There are 80,000 of us right now, not to mention all the people who've been involved in the company and are now no longer part of it."

That was the real genesis of this book I'd dreamt about since the day I almost knocked over a man in shirtsleeves hidden among some garments in an Arteixo store. He gave me that lovely idiosyncratic smile of his and said, "I'm Ortega, and you must be Covadonga. I've been expecting you." What neither of us suspected was how much of what we shared in the journey of our lives would be revealed. We both realised we had no right to keep secrets, however unimportant most of them might have seemed, yet they could be redolent of that intangible value addressed in the marketplace so frequently and giving rise to products from the luxury category. I'd be pleased if I could set down the story of that boy born in a town in León (a province of northwest Spain) 75 years ago and his mighty handmade empire for all to read.

1

My meeting with Amancio Ortega

"Just call me Ortega, and don't stand on ceremony"

The first impressions we have of a visit we've looked forward to, to visit an unforgettable city or person, are recorded in a certain way on the hard disks in our brains. They persevere with hints of an unrepeatable clarity, remaining unchanged even with time's passing and the thousands of things that happen in a life. That's how it was the day I met Amancio Ortega, nearly 15 years ago. It was December first, and the nineties were just beginning. Let me explain some background to give you a picture.

At the time I was the director of *Telva*, the leading magazine in Spain and always in the vanguard of what was happening in the world of fashion. I met and very often did business with some of the best designers from Paris, Milan, New York and London, places I visited at least twice a year for the collections. I hardly need to add that I was also to be found at the Cibeles and Gaudí catwalks, where the Madrid and Barcelona shows were held at the start of autumn and spring, respectively. In January and July it was Paris that surprised the world with its display of *haute couture* aesthetics. Its explosion of creativity and imagination were presented in the most sophisticated media, with the unmistakable glamour of French fashion that had dictated standards from the opening of the 20th century to the 1960s – standards accepted by the elite in all the greatest fashion capitals.

At that time, the name Zara was gathering momentum, but always with question marks. What lay behind that amazing phenomenon that the most recalcitrant fashion victims of the eighties and the beginning of the nineties were aiming at? How could you define this style of dress that didn't cost an arm and a leg, where the background music had a certain feeling of apology, of disposability, clearly bound to the consumer society in which we were all immersed? What was the source of the success of a fashion style that linked an attractive quality/price ratio with unmistakable echoes of design from the current top of the range? "It's an Armani design just for you", a professional in the field, an expert in luxury brands once said to me, convinced that he was right when he saw me wearing a perfectly made Zara jacket of impeccable cut and fabric characteristic of the great designer. That jacket was one of the first garments I bought from Zara, a store that was set to become, as for so many women, one of my favourite shops.

Very soon the recognisable black, unobtrusive bag with lettering in a dark, sandy shade sporting only its name as its logo was appearing in the streets of Europe's largest cities. Women who always wore the latest and stylists from international fashion magazines carried it with the same confidence as they would have if they were the latest trends from Prada, Gucci or Dior. What was most surprising was the skill with which women, who were famous as glamour icons, were beginning to combine – and praise – luxury brand clothing with Zara basics. This was later followed by the entire world. Even stories in magazines like *Telva, Elle, Marie Claire* or *Vogue* carried photographs of these emblematic women with items from the same brand.

Once again my newshound's nose led me to investigate this emerging phenomenon, which on top of everything else seemed shrouded in all kinds of suggestion and mystery. The least of these was that Zara was accused of copying; plagiarising the most outstanding aspects of each season's trends. There was talk about money laundering, murky business deals and strange secrets; there was a person with no face, someone who never appeared in the press, someone whose name was known but nothing more. Stories abounded that he was a peculiar individual who started his business making quilted dressing gowns at the start of the sixties, and without a word of explanation from anybody, had set out to conquer the most difficult fashion markets in the world.

Just what, exactly, was happening in Finisterre, the source of endless legends of witches emerging from the fog at the Coast of Death? Finisterre is on the rocky Costa da Morte (in Galician: "Coast of Death"), named because of the large number of shipwrecks along these shores. How could we find out the truth about what was happening in that part of northeastern Spain that had spawned so many of our fashion gurus – brothers Adolfo and Javier Domínguez, Antonio Pernas, Roberto Verino, Kina Fernández, Caramelo – that compelled people to talk about "Galician Fashion"? We had a right to a straight answer for the mountains of questions surrounding this mystery.

I sent a terrific journalist from the *Telva* team to find out. She had a sixth sense, the soul of a sleuth, and a huge gift for the kind of job that lies between pure, tough investigation and a whodunit, should those talents be required. She came back from her visit to Arteixo very excited about what she discovered, how she was received, the great business she uncovered and how she saw its prospects for the future. In April of that year, 1990, we published what was to be the first article on Zara under the headline "Zaramania", with the byline of Teresa Olazábal. "Cheek by jowl with *haute couture* firms, Zara has opened its shops on the best streets of Madrid, Paris, New York, Lisbon, Athens and Mexico City. The secret? An amazing capacity to sense fashion trends, take them on board and turn them into reality at bargain basement prices. And all within 20 days!" Underneath a list of data and figures relating to that period, that you would now have to multiply by several orders of magnitude, emphasis was placed on the fact that "in record time, this Galician company has turned into a holding company with 42 firms in its stable. They source its fabrics, dye them, print them, cut out the patterns, make them up and handle their distribution. At some stages of the process, Inditex organised 6,000 Galician village women into cooperatives to make up the garments. Yet Zara remains a mystery to many. Nobody understands how the clothes can be so inexpensive, how the designs match a number of fashion classics, or how the stocks are continually replenished."

What was the secret of his success? That was what everybody was wondering at the time, and they are still wondering. The answer was contained in four amazing lines uttered by one of the company managers: "From prices on, the entire process is undertaken without middlemen or agents. Apart from buying materials at good prices and using low-priced labour," he continued, "the business formula rests on a very small profit margin. We prefer to make a small amount from each item, but to sell a great many."

Another fundamental feature was to offer clothing in the latest designs. A designer on the team explained that the greatest success of the brand was based on swiftly sensing and interpreting fashion trends and customer tastes. "Inditex has a 40 person department," (how many would it be now, I wonder) "spread out through New York clubs, Parisian business districts and Spain's bars and fashionable venues. We call this trend-assessing procedure 'market testing with the target public'."

In my quest for more reasons for its all around success, I would add one factor that I think is crucial: constant renewal of stock, 40% of which is changed every week. Meantime, stock in the stores is replenished every three days. In other words, while other firms manufacture their collection only once for an entire season, Zara never stops changing its products to suit what people ask for.

As an obvious example, I include here the fact that I unfortunately witnessed the terrible events involving the Twin Towers in New York, known as 9/11. New York's fashion week had just opened, and on the afternoon before that date forever engraved in the history of the world, the 10th, a number of shows from American creators were presented. The new offerings were in the display windows of top stores in Manhattan, trends leaning towards a great deal of colour and hinting at a happy, fun-filled summer. When the catastrophe occurred, it wasn't just the Big Apple, but a sizable part of the world that went down under the terrorist attack. I shall never forget the pain and confusion that reigned in the streets, nor the black crepe that draped display windows indicating mourning, even at the most luxurious stores on main shopping streets, as well as in Soho or Tribeca, the most desirable districts. Everybody who had designed and produced a collection vibrant with colour saw their business paralysed for the season following the disaster. Grim though the shock was, it was exacerbated still further by the dominant colours which followed.

Shortly after, around Christmas time, back in New York for a few days I was able to confirm that during the previous months only Zara had continued to sell. This was because while in no way failing to share in the sadness and suffering of so many, thanks to its record production times it had filled its stores with dark, quiet shades appropriate to the tragedy the West was living through, above all in the area that bore the brunt of the horror that not only shook the concrete of the towers, but also a large proportion of humanity.

Olazábal concluded her story in *Telva* with an explanation that "data, figures and surprises apart, the most interesting thing about Zara is that it is turning into a social phenomenon. We are beginning to define Zaramania in people as a shopping habit: buying the latest fashion to wear and discard next year with a clear conscience." Something very serious lay at the heart of this observation: it revealed a genuine fashion revolution. Until about 20 years ago, fashion always appeared for the autumn-winter or spring-summer cycles and the best models were practically eternal. I can still remember Valentino in his workshop in Rome, explaining what it meant to him when some of his multimillionaire customers told him that one of his garments was still perfect after three or four years, and that it would then be preserved at the back of the wardrobe the way a priceless possession would be kept, perhaps even for their daughters. Is there anyone who would not look after a Pertegaz suit with something close to veneration, to say nothing of the Balenciaga that belonged to your grandmother or mother-in-law and that remained perfect, untouched by the passage of time?

Even so, it was another revolutionary, Paul Poiret, who claimed as long ago as 1890 that "the *raison d'être* of the clothing industry is novelty." This is the crucial factor that a far-seeing genius, Amancio Ortega, focused on a century later, dragging his entire team onto the dizzy locomotive of fashion to turn novelty delivered at the speed of sound in line with the 'just-in-time' theory, a keynote of his business identity and a new business model.

As a result of that article, the *Telva* publication team received letters from the most disparate centres of the world. Everybody wanted to be certain that what the journalist Teresa Olazábal had said was true. Best of all was a call to my office of a rather confidential nature from Milan. Someone very close to Giorgio Armani was wondering how contact could be made with Mr Ortega's "general HQ". They were very keen to talk with him. I do know that some conversations took place between the managers of the two companies, and it is very possible that visits were paid by managers of the Galician company to the capital of Italian fashion. But if the privacy of the Inditex founder is a deep mystery, all the more so have been his projects. They talked, they exchanged impressions, they carried out the odd financial study but nobody revealed the real content of the conversations. "Sure, we were in contact. And not just with Armani", I was told on one of the occasions when I asked. Although I have no sound reason for thinking so, I always suspected that the backers behind the Armani empire were aware of the fact that quality garments with a similar feel were being seen in the streets of various cities of Europe and they were bought at a third or a quarter of his prices. So why not organise a joint venture or some mutual project? I repeat that such ideas at the time were pure guesswork, never confirmed, never denied. It was years later, as I shall recount in due course, that I found out what actually happened.

1 December 1990

The flight from Madrid to La Coruña took off from Barajas airport and landed at the Galician airport with British punctuality. We were welcomed by a typical north-western Spanish day: clouds coming and going, moments of sunshine and fine rain that turns the fields into meadows containing every shade of green. In the background, the Cantabrian Sea, sometimes very rough, was smooth and calm.

Everything seemed to augur well. I was travelling with Montse Cuesta, chief fashion editor on the magazine and now the editor of *Architectural Digest*. With all the excitement of the explorers who landed in America, we arrived at our destination prepared to dispel the collection of mysteries that veiled Inditex, the company that spread through the world like wildfire, silent but unstoppable. We met its founder and driving force, an enigma about whom practically everybody had an opinion yet so little was known, not even what he looked like. This was true, I was later told by one of his friends, that one morning when they happened to be in a bar in La Coruña they heard someone claiming to know Ortega, unaware that the very person he was talking about was the unsophisticated-looking character drinking coffee at his side. There was no shortage of people who couldn't distinguish between imagining they knew Amancio and reality. The fact is that man who bid fair to become the personality of the century was beginning to turn into a very important target to aim for.

The programme that was prepared for us at head office consisted of a thorough exploration of the plant, precise explanations about the company, lunch with the chairman and then back to Madrid. We felt we had won the Christmas lottery, and were still clutching our winning tickets as we walked down the aircraft steps.

A driver met us in the airport waiting room, ready to drive us to the Inditex head office in the Sabón industrial zone. One of the management team welcomed us and asked us to follow him. From that day on, every time I have had the opportunity of visiting I have been reminded that it is not only the clothing that emerges from this huge industrial network that has its own stamp, but also the people who work there. They are kind, welcoming and well-mannered. Inditex has an authentic business culture. The various "professors" from this company who have taught MBA classes at ISEM Fashion Business School in Madrid in recent years, currently under my leadership, have motivated the students to be as moved by the quality of their shows as by the friendliness and respect that they are treated with. From José María Castellano, who now sits on our Advisory Board and who gave a number of talks when he was Vice-President and CEO of Inditex, to the directors of Zara Home, Logística, and Mercado de Capitales, the general secretary or current Vice-President and CEO,

Pablo Isla, everybody shares an unmistakable sense of know-how and awareness of what it means to be a part of a company like this. They are also all aware of the importance of teamwork, which always gets a special mention in their lectures.

When our students pay a study visit to Arteixo, they come back thrilled by the business complex they discover, although they also learn a great deal from the impeccable manners of their hosts such as Communications Head, Jesús Echevarría, or other executives. This special way of behaving and communicating what the company means is difficult to define, but clear to outside observers.

In the case of our own visit, by mid-morning we were walking through the different sections in which the complex task of putting together the garments takes place before they are sent off to their various destinations. The ceiling is criss-crossed by rails along which the mass-produced clothing endlessly travels in an orderly manner on its way to the labelling, ironing and packaging zones and finally, to the point where the rails divide according to which store will be their final destination. In this final step, sophisticated and efficient machines fold jackets, blouses or trousers and place them in huge cardboard boxes. If the garment cannot be folded and has to travel upright, it is put onto hangers that are automatically inserted into special containers. On each of the boxes the shop's address can be read, whether somewhere in Spain or in another country such as France or Portugal. Even then, the Zara empire had crossed the first European borders.

Fascinated by this endless motion and the ultra-modern machinery with hardly a sign of the human beings who controlled them, Montse and I are surprised by the appearance of a smiling, friendly man in shirtsleeves crossing the section from a cloud of overcoats. He watched us with surprise and pleasure at our presence. No doubt he'll be the foreman of the section I thought. I stepped forward to greet him and told him how astonished we were by everything we saw that morning.

I can't say I clearly remember, but I presume I said we were journalists from Madrid, invited by Mr Ortega to visit the factory.

We immediately added that our main concern was to meet the person who had been able to start up what now appeared to be an unprecedented success. In response to my enthusiastic comments, and in a not particularly Galician accent, although with the sarcasm so well known in those parts he asked me, "So you'd like to meet Ortega, would you?" The well-known official photograph could have saved us a few minutes of doubt but it had not yet been launched. "Well, dears," and that's a word I've heard so many, many times over the years I've been fortunate enough to know him, "here you have him. I'm Ortega." Amused by our surprise, he quickly added, "This has really been a chance encounter; I assure you it wasn't planned. I spend a lot of time moving from one area of the factory to another to see how everything is working. If I'm not in the warehouse, then I'll be in design. Frankly, the entire process fascinates me – but I really love seeing what our artists come up with! That's my favourite side of the entire complex."

That was our introduction. It would now be superfluous to add that everybody who has had hands-on dealings with him or has worked at his side is in agreement about how certain aspects are immediately apparent in the first meeting: transparency, lack of sophistication and passion for the work. Everything I have been able to learn about both the man and the way he constructed the business I picked up in just a few seconds.

Unwilling to waste a moment of our time, I asked, "When you talk to the designers, Mr Ortega, do you let them know your opinions?" He replied, "Before we go any further, just one thing – no more 'Mr Ortega' please. Here I'm just Ortega, and that's for everybody." Increasingly surprised by his casual attitude, I introduced Montse Cuesta to him. He seemed delighted by us and immediately turned into the perfect host. "I'll take you around the factory myself." Just before we started, he repeated, "Just call me Ortega; never stand on ceremony."

I would have preferred to use his Christian name, and straightaway I said that since he was the only Amancio I knew if he was comfortable with it, then that was what I would call him. It really seemed that the first conversation was not going to be the last and that we would have many further occasions to meet, chat and exchange impressions, not just about the business, but about the thousand and one other matters that concerned him and filled his thoughts and day-to-day operations. What I achieved with my "exclusivity" is that every time I call him, when I ask "How are you, Amancio?" he immediately recognises me and replies in the friendliest of tones. He finds it amusing that I don't address him by his surname like everybody else does, even his family. When sending him my best wishes on New Year's Eve for example, I never fail to get real pleasure from telling him that I'm thinking about him fondly and wishing even greater success in the upcoming year than in previous years. His reply is usually the same, "And my prayers are for health for everybody and for things to at least go on as before. Naturally, if they're better, then so much the better for everybody." It makes no difference whether the calendar shows a change of year or that a new millennium is starting, as happened in 2000, a time when all kinds of crazy things were going on to celebrate. Amancio had not set off for some exotic location – he was still at his home in La Coruña. Indeed, at the end of that morning as I sent my best wishes and asked, "What are you up to? How will you welcome in the new millennium?" he answered, "What would I be doing? Working, of course; if I want everything to keep on working, I shall have to battle on, whatever happens."

On that morning when we met he just took over the leadership of the group. He wanted to know what we had seen so far and he piloted us to the zones we had yet to visit. We made our way to another section where a team of Danish engineers were fitting some IT installations that were very advanced for the time. We stopped to listen and watch what they were doing. Although we didn't understand the language we could certainly admire the way they handled those glittering machines destined to revolutionise the market with groundbreaking programmes, programmes that were mysterious to anybody not at the forefront of the technology. Ortega's smile was a picture when he saw us literally open-mouthed at the futuristic scene that lay before us. I may not have understood too much of the highly complex machinery they were showing us, but I did suspect that it was here that a considerable proportion of the secrets of this company, destined to lead the world textile industry, were to be found and were being shaped.

Ortega's dream which he shared with the group of managers with which he worked, was to achieve nothing less than the best logistics system in the world; an unprecedented formula that would allow him to place a product in a store, regardless of its location, in under a fortnight. This was what he focused on with devotion. In other words, it would be a complete change in the world of retail and distribution.

We continued our visit. In one large room furnished with huge drafting tables, a group of designers were at work surrounded by dozens of international magazines, mostly fashion, but some of the coffee table variety we were just beginning to call "lifestyle" magazines. One wall was flanked by a line of coat hangers loaded with garments. I moved over to take a look and saw some labels and famous names. My eyes met those of Ortega. Very quickly, candidly and clearly he gave me an explanation I certainly hadn't asked for, "Obviously, we are going to be inspired by what people accept and look for on the world market! Here we study the garments, take them apart, draw them, put them back together again, adapt them to our own style, make them up and launch them onto the market."

While listening to him – and the same thing happens every time I recall that very graphic scene – I think about the great Balenciaga, the frame of reference for the best designers in the world. At the start of his career he once travelled to Paris, and together with sketches he himself made after each collection, gaining inspiration from what he had just seen, he bought some of the models from the collections in order to study them and make his own creations along the lines of the period's top designer masterpieces. This was recounted to me by his great friend and greatest admirer, Hubert de Givenchy, with whom he shared years of work and friendship; he also told me that Cristóbal never made mistakes when it came to choosing what to buy. "He was always right," he explained on one occasion in his Paris home, talking of the beginnings of Balenciaga's career in an almost reverential tone. "Back in Spain, in his San Sebastián workshop, before he moved to his premises in George V in Paris, Cristóbal would take apart those models – we would call them prototypes now – and become completely absorbed in each one. That was how he learned how the top creators of the time cut on the bias, cut a sleeve, set the shoulders correctly and placed the stitching perfectly, etc. This was the more technical side. To this he added his innovation, talent and creativity." That was his school of design – his personal academy of fine arts, and to this he added his contemplation of the Cantabrian Sea in contrast with the jagged mountains and the foothills of the Pyrenees that the artist could see from his hometown of Guetaria. It was a landscape that filled his eyes with a certain chiaroscuro that he then expressed in his designs and turned into dresses of extraordinary colours and outlines.

That day I realised that this group of designers camped on the coast of Galicia on the same Cantabrian Sea were learning and being inspired in that same school, led by "Captain" Ortega.

The trends, colours and successes for every season arrived at the design tables in Arteixo from everywhere in Europe and beyond. This was always this man's obsession: clothing that was redeveloped and reworked in direct relation to what consumers wanted and garments that appeared swiftly to hang in Madrid, Barcelona and other Spanish cities as well as in Porto, Paris or Mexico City.

When we had listened to him for some time I asked, "Would it be possible to take a photograph?" He was in his shirtsleeves without a tie and looking just like a workman but that wasn't why he refused. Very gently and quietly (in the 20 years I have known him I have never known him to raise his voice) he firmly replied "Absolutely not!" I realised that his determination to protect his privacy had not changed one iota, but I explained that there was no reason for him to worry, as this would not be a photograph for publication. Indeed, we were not producing a photo story. I simply wanted a memento of someone whose capacity for work, vision of the future and simplicity, as the genius Cervantes would say, I found delightful.

Amancio was listening to me with that smile that he almost always wore, making a very idiosyncratic gesture that suggested I should keep talking, but that I had almost won him over. To add a convincing reason it occurred to me to tell him that in my professional life I had met a number of people who were of great interest because of their work and contribution to the world, and that I liked to have some visual evidence of my meetings with them. "For example," I said, "I have a photo of me with the king, an astronaut, a Nobel laureate plus others I see as important and exemplary. I certainly wouldn't want them to appear in the press – I just want to preserve a memory of a moment that is historical for me."

He hesitated for a few seconds. "Look, if we do this photograph with you on the grounds of your argument, well, I'd like to have a copy as a memento, too. And then I'd think, why not take one with somebody else, and then somebody else, and so on? And that's the end of my privacy. The only people I want to recognise me in the street are my family, friends and workmates. I'm trying to live a quiet life, be just another person, be able to go where I want, have a coffee on the terrace on María Pita Square – a traditional setting in La Coruña – or take a stroll along the promenade without everybody knowing who I am."

I told him that I always made every effort to respect the decisions of others. He was unruffled and carried on showing us the various workshops. His careful explanations of the smallest details showed that he knew the business inside out. He never stopped being fully involved in it, tirelessly playing his part in the work and monitoring the production chain, step by step. The things he told us were easy to observe; what was complicated was managing to conceive of a formula that could successfully handle this perfectly organised system of distribution at such a rapid rate.

It may be that our careers are such that we meet few people; but what drew my attention was that Amancio knew every worker by name. He had a friendly word for everyone.

The end of the visit

When we finished the tour we went to eat at the Gallo de Oro, a restaurant close by where Amancio used to take his guests before the company opened its own restaurant in the main offices. We took a seat in his favourite corner at a very ordinary table.

Before checking the menu and with a look of concern, he asked, "Did that business about the photo bother you?" It was obvious that he was slightly uncomfortable about it, given that in his philosophy of life one important feature was to be as pleasant as he could to those around him, whoever they might be. Once again he apologised, adding the same explanation as he had given me before. It was only when I stressed the fact that I respected his position that he added: "These baby eels are almost as good as those from the part of Spain where you come from." I ordered them and discovered that his concern for excellence was not restricted to his entrepreneurial activities.

Lunch was a delight, and we chatted about scores of things, including one I frequently recall. Even then I remember that I thought Zara clothes were very good, particularly because of the perfect quality-price ratio. It happened that on that day I was wearing a Zara brand suit in grey flannel, perfectly cut. I told him, and he said that he had immediately recognised it, that he liked to see me in one of his garments – not because it was his, but because he felt very satisfied to see that customers liked his products. I took the opportunity to add several comments about what I liked about the company but then he broke in. "Listen," he said, "I'm going to ask you to do me a favour. Tell me what there is that you don't like about Zara now. I already know from Elena" – the manager of the Velázquez store in Madrid – "that you're a good customer, that you understand fashion and you run a very good magazine. Yours is the kind of opinion that matters to me and I would value any criticism you might make about something I could do better."

I took him at his word and prepared to reply as clearly as I could. The truth is, that despite his insistence, I wasn't very happy about telling him anything negative on the very day I met him and in the middle of a meal where I was the guest. But he asked so nicely that I told him what I thought. "In my opinion – and not just mine, either – the knitwear is not particularly well-made and while the footwear is often well designed, the material is as hard as a rock. I hardly dare even try on the footwear!"

He made no note of this; another of his outstanding qualities that everybody agrees about is his remarkable memory. He never forgets the slightest thing about anything that matters; he always listens with interest and sooner or later he will make use of what is stored in his brain. I was able to witness that a few months ago on one of my recent visits to Arteixo. On that day I was wearing a pair of shoes I'd bought from Zara, not because I was visiting Amancio, but because they were so comfortable that I had hardly taken them off throughout the entire winter.

I showed them to him, and to my surprise he said that he perfectly remembered my negative comment during that first lunch many years before. He repeated almost the same words I had used. To highlight the difference between my comment at that time and the situation today he said, "Did you know that Princess Matilde of the Belgians has an identical pair? I saw them in a photograph in a magazine. They really suited her." His face hardly changed as he said this. But what gave him huge satisfaction was to know that the team now making his footwear in the Tempe factory (in Alicante) were producing satisfied customers everywhere in the world.

2

First Steps in a Story

Remembering his parents

"My father's wage was 300 pesetas (less than two euros today). And don't start telling me that at the time it wasn't too bad, because it wouldn't keep a family then any more than it will now. There were three children, Antonio, the eldest, Pepita, the only girl and me, the baby. And that wage was never enough to make it to the end of the month."

We were having lunch, one of the many I have been lucky enough to share with Amancio Ortega to discuss a range of work-related subjects. We were in the guests' dining room at the new Arteixo head offices. At one end of the room is a very comfortable area with a couch and coffee table where you can have an aperitif before eating. Everything has a feeling of good taste and minimalist simplicity, one of the features of the entire building. White tablecloths, perfect white crockery and a menu that pays homage to the country: seafood and fish such as grouper, monkfish or hake, prepared to perfection. While the desserts might not fit in with this *haute cuisine* class, they were special too.

As a general rule, Amancio is not a huge eater but he is an excellent host. "My favourite meal," he told me more than once, s fried eggs, chips and chorizo sausage". Still very down-to-earth, incapable of putting on airs, never mind his frequent mentions in international financial papers as one of the richest men in Spain. He is included in *Forbes'* list of the world's richest people and importance increases as the years pass. He told me every detail of the starting point of his life in business; a story so unusual and touching, so profoundly human, a vital testimony to his life.

There were three of us dining together: Amancio, then CEO José María Castellano and me. We chatted about a thousand different things in that lengthy conversation dotted with his unique memories, fragments that illuminated his life's panorama and remained fresh in his memory despite the passing years. Fortunately, they have remained vivid in mine, too. When we touched on the spectacular growth Inditex had undergone, rather amazing in the light of the future that the nineties seemed to offer, I asked him with genuine curiosity what the first steps of such a remarkable phenomenon had been. Even then a number of different versions of the origin of his business dealings had already appeared in print, but I never imagined I was to have the opportunity of hearing from the horse's mouth the most profound motivation, the stimulus that moved Amancio to launch his conquest of the textiles business. He was fired by the same idealism and taste for danger that inspired so many heroes centuries ago to accomplish their great deeds in the discovery of America, from Columbus to Hernán Cortés. Slowly, as though reliving each second of his most intimate experiences, those that lie hidden in the secret corners of our souls and are preserved there like buried treasure, he began to tell us a story of something that happened when he was still a child, just about to take that awkward step into adolescence. His account provides much food for thought about the way need, hunger or a tough situation can be the launching pad for professional, political, religious or personal successes that are scribed in the golden book of the story of humanity. This brings to mind something that Luis Miguel Dominguín (a legendary bullfighter) told me many years ago when he was at the peak of his career. His son, then just a child, was playing in the garden of his home at Somosaguas (an elegant "barrio" or neighbourhood close to Madrid), "That kid will never be a bullfighter. To go up against a bull, you have to know the meaning of hunger." Could hunger be the force that drives a genius, a hero or a saint to reach for the stars?

Here is what Amancio told us: "I remember one afternoon after school when I went with my mother to buy some food. I was the youngest, remember, and she liked coming to meet me after school to bring me home. Quite often I would be with her when she went to do the shopping. The shop we went to was one of those big grocer's of that time with a very high counter, so high in fact, that I could never see who was talking to my mother but I heard a man's voice say something that despite the passage of time I have never forgotten, 'Josefa, I'm very sorry, but I can't let you have any more credit.' I was shocked. I was just 12."

Amancio went on to explain that he was a very sensitive child with a strong sense of honour, and when he had gotten over the words he had just heard he decided that he would always stand by her. "This was the last time this would ever happen to my mother. I saw the situation very clearly and from that day on I would find work to earn money and help the household. I dropped out of school, gave up my studies and got myself a job as a sales assistant in a shirtmaker's." That business is still in La Coruña, on the corner of Juan Flórez Street.

Years later I told Amancio how much I had been impressed by what he said, how much I had thought about his account of his first steps on that long road and how he never rested, never lost his energy for being a tireless worker. On that occasion he firmly reiterated that once he had set the course he never once regretted it; he also never allowed himself to forget his humble origins and that awful event in his childhood when they lacked the basic means they needed to feed themselves. There was no doubt that it had helped forge a character capable of tackling the endless difficulties that beset every day of many people's lives.

The underlying truth of this anecdote, like any other about the beginnings of his professional and life career, is that this conqueror of the international retail world, the man who provokes enormous curiosity and huge admiration most definitely threw himself unconditionally into the university of life. What is awe-inspiring about this is that after many decades of "attending class", he still never misses a day. He has never taken a sabbatical year and he still wins top marks in all the international competitions.

Amancio never doubted that if he wanted to win a degree with sound value in the university of fashion he would have to earn it through effort, stamina and enthusiasm that needed renewing every day. These are all the essential ingredients for someone about to tackle a task such as that taken on by this visionary. Who could have guessed that the 12-year-old at the store would be the cement of a genuinely revolutionary business? From that crucial moment when still clutching his mother's hand he abandoned childhood and set about the business of keeping his family fed while finding himself on step one as a wage-earner in a small local business.

Amancio Ortega is a man whose truest reality is unknown to nearly everyone; a human being with flashing eyes, moist at the emotion of the memory, concealing the unforgettable scar of a child wounded by scorn and the awful reality of their lives. Or maybe he's just a boy who rebelled against the want of essentials and who took the courageous step of turning the situation around once and for all. With the greatest honesty and simplicity, he recognised that he could never in his wildest dreams have imagined what was to happen in his life after that premature decision to abandon his textbooks.

The outcome of that decision was that he began to develop a great natural intelligence; he became one of those people that history rarely sees, possessed of a will of iron for ensuring the completion of tasks great and small or to build something wonderful from the endless seemingly trivial issues that stack on top of each other and are dealt with every day. As the Catalan singer-songwriter Joan Manuel Serrat says, "There is no road – we build it as we travel."

There is no doubt that from the moment he began his career as the least important employee at the shirtmaker's until now, he set aside many of the opportunities life offers to billionaires. Amancio Ortega elected to devote himself body and soul to the business that he was slowly discovering and in which he continues to be so deeply involved. "Everybody has a purpose," is something you will hear him repeat with the absolute conviction of a person with a mission. While his starting point, the first brick in the colossal building he erected, might have been to help his family, what motivates him now is not simply making money. However valid that may be for an aspiring businessman, it is not enough for him. He is moved by an idea that illuminates an important aspect of his biography, "It's something more profound that drives me to work, and that has done so since that day when I was still a child. It isn't money, essential though that may be. There are other, different reasons that I came to discover, all justified, that led me to carry on tirelessly. I might as well have started work when I was 13, because I was there a year before they registered me, since I was too young. I treasure the first contract I had from Gala (the first clothing shop where he worked)."

He continues the story, his eyes reflecting nostalgia and strength, further aspects of his character that mark his personal and professional career. His eyes reveal who he is and hint at the people who stood by him at each stage of his life, including why he never stopped fighting, regardless of the cost.

"When I was a child, I hated being sneered at. When I was 9, 10, 11, I was very emotional, I felt everything. I've never raised my voice because I don't like making others feel bad, but I must tell you that I was very proud. When I was a little older, working at La Maja (the next clothing shop where he worked), which was classier than my previous job, I once strolled through La Coruña with the daughter of one of the customers, a rather wealthy lady. It looked as though that girl was in love with the boy who worked in the shop – me, in other words. It even made *me* smile.

"One day the girl's mother came into the shop and asked the boss where his son Amancio was. Of course, the owner said that I wasn't his son, and you could see the displeasure in the mother's expression. She really didn't like the idea that I might be going out with her daughter. What, just because I was a mere shop assistant and not the owner's son? That had a profound effect on me. When I remember that time, I think that rich people then were different, not the way I believe a person with money ought to be. They were much more insular and they guarded their money jealously – and even though there might not have been a huge amount of it, it gave them that feeling of exclusivity. I really suffered because of what happened; it was very hurtful to a teenager.

"From that day onwards I've always tried to bear people's feelings in mind and to save those close to me from being hurt as I had been."

Despite this "incident" he still maintained a very clear idea of what he intended to do, and never thought of studying for a degree like someone with intellectual and social cachet. He was committed to achieving his goal: "I had no time to study because I was working around the clock. My perception of what I wanted to do became clearer and clearer and I couldn't stop until I was in a position to launch the idea with others involved. What I really regret after such a long time is that I never learned to speak English, because I can see how essential it is. But what I lack because of it I can learn from listening a great deal and learning from people around me."

The way he describes this is very impressive when you consider that students in business school idolize him. He remains a great mystery to so many businessmen who have invested precious years of their lives in preparation for the future. With all the simplicity in the world he says that the foundations of his professional training have been life and the work itself. He is almost under an obligation to describe how the Ortega of today is different from that young shop assistant who objected to injustice and who was never daunted by the toughness of life.

"I can assure you that I basically haven't changed. My thinking is the same now as it was then. What matters is setting yourself goals in life and putting everything you have into reaching them.

"From the time I started working I was obsessed by one idea – why shouldn't I invent something different from everything else on the market? I could see very clearly that I wanted to fill a space that existed in the world of the textile industry. I wouldn't be able to clearly define what I was thinking about at that time, but I decided to follow that impulse and I set up GOA with my brother Antonio. We opened an account with 2,500 pesetas (less than 20 euros today). My sister-in-law, who could sew, and my first wife, Rosalía, were making the famous quilted dressing gowns that were so fashionable at the time."

Among the memories I have of our conversations and meetings, there is another moment that defines Amancio as the unique human being he is, naturally with all his pros and cons as with any other mortal. When speaking of that intuition that drove him to launch a different way of working, I asked him how he planned Inditex, the company that he transformed into the largest textile group in the world. His philosophy and sound fundamentals are obvious in every sentence he utters. He speaks without haste, thinking carefully about what he says. The reasons that drive his life are very clear to him.

"In my case, from the very beginning, I've given everything to the job, however demanding it might be. I've never been satisfied with what I was doing and I've tried to inculcate that into the people I work with. Self-satisfaction is a terrible trap if you want to achieve anything important. In this company we've never rested on our laurels, not when we were taking our first steps nor now, when we have shops everywhere in the world. Blind optimism is a mistake. You must always want to do better and never lose the ability to criticise yourself. I always felt that if we were going to win, we had to be stretched every day. But I should tell you that this business is less complicated than it looks. It's very easy to manage."

In that atmosphere of encouraging confidences, I couldn't resist the temptation to find out more about the empire and the "emperor". It is only by listening to Amancio in person, that you can gain a better understanding of what we know today. To achieve this, we must take a step back into the past, to investigate how the man spent the first years of his life.

Tracing his roots

Many people think that Amancio Ortega, based in Finisterre, was born in Galicia. We have the picture of a misty morning on the northeastern coast peopled by cockle-pickers and fishermen out on the shores while their women are home, devoting their time to sewing in a workshop for small businessmen who will later become famous. It seems natural to assume that the driving force and soul of an empire like that in the days of Philip II, King of Spain during the 16th century, "on which the sun never set," should have lived and worked since he was a child at this end of the peninsula as a local on native soil.

Few witnesses now remain, but documentary evidence shows that Amancio Ortega was born in a village in León, Busdongo de Arbás, on the southern flank of Pajares Pass on the border between León and Asturias. The population of the village is 1,300 and it possesses a coal mine and a cement factory. Those who have investigated his roots say that Amancio was born on 28 March 1936, just a few months before the outbreak of the Spanish Civil War; that he shares his birthday with Peruvian author Mario Vargas Llosa, and other alleged facts of that nature that Amancio finds amusing. What he told me with genuine pride and admiration for the high quality of his work is that his father "was a railwayman, a native of Valladolid. When I was born he had been sent to this village as an interlocking fitter, which meant his job was to monitor the condition of the points and track, and he was assiduous in his work."

So vivid is his memory of his father and so great the influence he had on various aspects of his character, that on one occasion when we had an appointment for a certain time that he had to postpone because of some unforeseen circumstance, he apologised a number of times. When I said, "Please, Amancio, it happens to everybody, don't mention it," he replied that for his father, a railwayman, punctuality was a crucial aspect of his day-to-day work, and he inculcated it into his family. "I hate missing an appointment and I'm even less fond of being late. That's what I learned from my father, among other things."

Shortly after, when young Amancio was only three months old, the family moved to a paper-making town, Tolosa, a few kilometres from San Sebastián. He vividly recalls his mother's home village, Valoria la Buena, where they spent summer holidays and Holy Week. So sweet are the memories and such is the admiration he feels for his mother that his yacht bears the name of his mother Josefa's birthplace, Valoria. The years he spent in the Basque country and his childhood memories have also left marks that are difficult to erase: the college of monks where he went to study, his escapades in the orchards, stealing apples and pears and like all little boys, typical village pranks that make him laugh out loud when he calls them to mind.

In August 1944 his father was transferred to La Coruña where a railway branch was being built on the line from Santiago to Zamora.

When Amancio, then eight, remembers that period of his childhood in Galicia, he finds himself contemplating a very tough part of the Spanish post-war years. When he casts his mind back, he says that he never heard the war mentioned in their home, yet his father must have had a very difficult time. "When the war broke out my parents were living in a very small village where some of their friends lived and died, and that sort of thing changes you."

In 1960 his father was promoted to gang head and awarded a prize for efficiency, and in 1971 he was appointed team leader, but decided to retire and along with his wife, enjoy something of what his children had done. Amancio becomes emotional when he thinks that his work helped give his parents some years of the peace and wellbeing he wanted them to have. He always remembers that terrible afternoon when he became brutally acquainted with lacking the basics in life. Fixed in his memory, like a living photograph, is the beginning of his working life at the Gala shirtmaker's. He recalls that it wasn't all tough times and there is pleasure in remembering what happened in his first job. "As you would expect, I was the general shop dogsbody. I cleaned the shop, made up packages and dealt with customers when we were busy. It seems that customers mentioned me to the boss because they noticed that from the moment I set foot in the shop I took the work very seriously and with a sense of responsibility. I always liked my work, and was very keen to learn."

After opening shop number 3,000 worldwide, the Inditex boss told me that he always understood very clearly that you must never lose sight of the customer. He had been outstanding in the shirt business because of how he dealt with everybody who came into the shop. That very serious, hard-working boy who was always ready to lend a hand to anyone who needed help is the same person today, at the age of 75, ready to pay attention to anyone who needs his opinion about solving a problem or spotlighting an important area of the dizzying international expansion on which the company is bent.

When I rang him on 28 March 2008 to wish him happy birthday, he turned out naturally enough, to be at work. He was delighted that I had remembered him, and when I asked, "Amancio, what are you doing today at Inditex instead of celebrating your birthday at home?"

I got the same answer I'd heard on other occasions: "Why stay home? I'm doing what I'm always doing, working. I did, however, come in a bit late today. As you know, my breakfast is always important – first I have something at home with the family and then I have a snack with my friends. It takes very little to make me happy."

"Did you ask for anything special on your birthday?"

"I just ask God for health to keep on going," he replied.

Before opening his own business, at the age of 17 Amancio left his first company and was taken on as an assistant at La Maja, quite a large business according to a friend of his sister Josefa. The company had several branches where his elder brother and sister, Antonio and Pepita, worked. When it happened that Amancio, advancing swiftly due to qualities that hinted he might be an effective businessman, was promoted to manager, the person who took his place was a girl of 16 called Rosalía Mera Goyenechea, whom he married two years later.

The owners of La Maja paid a great deal of attention to the suggestions made by the youngest Ortega. One was that he would take on the making up of garments using the shop's fabric and labour brought in by Primitiva, his brother Antonio's wife, a dressmaker. The results were satisfactory, and so Amancio, unwilling to give away the added value deriving from his initiatives, resigned from his job as a shop assistant to become a full-time manufacturer. In his 10 years of experience he made contact with Catalan textiles manufacturers who offered him wholesale prices and he built up a significant portfolio of his own customers.

Thus equipped and with the bank loan of 2,500 pesetas we mentioned before, he opened his own business, GOA Confecciones in 1963. The name came from the back-to-front initials of his forename and his brother Antonio's name, plus the two surnames. He was accompanied by his wife, her siblings and a great friend of the family, salesman José Cañas, future creator of the company Caramelo.

In order to get started they set up in a modest workshop and concentrated on making the famous women's quilted dressing gowns, which sold much better than they had expected. By reinvesting the majority of their earnings, Amancio Ortega got his workshop off on the right foot so he concentrated on making clothing that was sold to middlemen. He even succeeded in exporting a portion of the output. Ten years later his workforce was 500 strong, he had taken over the supply and distribution operations and he had contracted a team of designers. He was ready to take a leap into the one link in the chain he had not yet covered: retail distribution.

In 1975 the opening of the first Zara shop in La Coruña flagged the completion of a vertical integration procedure that represented a phenomenon unknown in the European fashion industry at that time. I learned from someone who worked in a workshop for this family team that the empire-builder in the making worked non-stop, in the early years, to expand his newborn brand, Zara, throughout Galicia. He set up other companies responsible for various production lines and accumulated the capital on which he based his fantasy some years later. "You'll notice that I don't have an office," Amancio told me in one of our conversations. "I've never had one. My work isn't paperwork, it's factory work." And it happens to be the truth that that's how I met him, peeking out from the dangling garments that moved around a carousel in his distribution shed.

Amancio is a creature of habit. This is how he describes his preferences each day, and it has been so for years, "What I like most is to spend time in the design area. I've always enjoyed being surrounded by creative people who are mostly young, and listen to their suggestions; people who spend their time travelling the world and noticing all the trends in the media, not just as regards clothing, but also lifestyles. You learn a great deal by listening to them. If they want my opinion they get it, but they're excellent professionals and they know what they're doing."

3

Zara: A New Fashion Culture Takes its Place in the 21st Century

"Even when I was nobody at all, I used to dream about growing the company"

In one of our conversations Amancio once said, "Someone who once paid a visit to the offices, a great business expert, told me that what I started was a groundbreaking, innovative textile distribution company." With that clear idea and without a single extra word, he summed up why this great company, the flagship in the sector, adopted the name 'Inditex'. "If he said it so enthusiastically, he must be right," thought Amancio, who never allowed his forward movement to be slowed down by details. "I could see my goals very clearly and I accepted that what was in progress and what had worked very well until that moment was a textile design industry." Thus the name was born naturally and without complications.

Alongside the first name of the tiny garment workshop referred to earlier, GOA, Ortega gave his *imprimatur* to the name Inditex for a company that a few short years later would be the eighth most successful company in the world. An article in *El País* on 16 June 2008 commented that, "the rise of Inditex has been spectacular. Only four years ago the GAP, the American leader at the time, was selling double the quantity of the Spanish group, which was number three behind the Swedish company H&M. By 2005,

45

it had become the European leader and in recent years its powerful growth has continued, while the GAP business has stagnated.

"The crisis that afflicted the US group that sells through the GAP, Banana Republic and Old Navy chains, became obvious to all at the beginning of this year with a 10 per cent drop in sales. That fact, plus the fall in the value of the dollar, has handed Inditex the gold medal on a platter, something that only a few years ago would have seemed impossible. This growth model has turned into the absolute winner as far as customer preferences are concerned."

As Amancio puts it, "what the company needed so much when we decided on the name as it appears today when we are so well positioned, was what we strove to give it every day, and we work to keep to the same course. My priority has always been the company, and I have done everything for it with utter dedication since day one. I can't repeat too often that everything I have done has been thanks to the people who so often imitated my dedication – which I do not deny, because I am a very ambitious individual. Even when I was nobody and hardly had a thing, I was dreaming about growing. We have never rested on our laurels or gone for the easy way out. Optimism can be a very negative emotion. You have to take risks! I never stopped saying it to everybody who joined the company. That meant sticking to what we had in mind with utter commitment. The handful of us who started this business were doing it from the start. Every day new ideas came up, and we never had any preconceived plans. Growth is a survival mechanism – without growth, a company dies. A company has to live for the benefit of the people who made a commitment to seeing that it grows. And now that I'm 72," he told me just three years ago, "I feel just the same. You can't stop growing."

Achieving pre-set goals has always been what drives the machinery of the company. This is a commitment that he has lived with passion, supported by visionary intelligence, intuition, his view of the future and hours of intense work. He spent two years, 1986 and 1987, ensuring that all the manufacturing companies in the group would direct all of their output to the Zara chain. During that time the fundamentals for a logistics system that could handle the predicted rapid rate of growth were established. This is a production system that has worked its way into the thinking of businesspeople of the 21st century, and is now being applied to other fields in the luxury and fashion world such as accessories, jewellery, cosmetics and others.

A student in Shanghai: "Everything is from Zara, my favourite shop."

Another successful strategy from the president of Inditex is his ability to adapt his view of fashion to the societal changes taking place. If you want to find out what is happening to the lifestyle that surrounds you, you should leaf through the pages of a good fashion magazine, soak up the trends and offerings, take a stroll through the streets where young people spend their time and enjoy themselves, and watch, watch, and never stop watching.

Now we live in the era of the internet, new technologies, and McLuhan's global village. An unmistakable characteristic of this new landscape is the way women are comfortably occupying every possible area of professional activity, happily certain that they can blend family life with an absorbing job. Time has become their most precious luxury. "I know that at Zara I shall always be able to find what I need, and I shan't have to spend hours searching," is something you will hear in every language under the sun.

The last time I was in Shanghai, attending a Prestige Brands Forum that was held at the CEIBS (China Europe International Business School), I took some time out to have a look at the city. I noticed upwards of 10 women with typical Asian features dressed in western styles coming out of a spectacular Zara store located as always, in the city's golden mile – carrying the characteristic Zara bag. One of our stewardesses, an MBA student at this business college was excellently dressed displaying, up-to-the-minute taste. When I asked where the clothing she was wearing came from, she was half amazed and half amused. "Everything is from Zara, my favourite shop," she replied.

The new roles taken by women in our globalised society are a reality that is profoundly changing in our ways of thinking and living. It is fashion that must fit in with this reality, not the other way round. Obviously in contrast with the showy materialism that characterised the eighties, the first decade of the new millennium has been characterised by a comfortable, minimalist clothing style that noticeably features simplicity and practicality. In this climate in which the *basics* rule, a good quality/price ratio is crucial. "At that price I can wear it for a season and then forget about it."

In the blink of an eye, a new way of understanding clothing that chimes much more harmoniously with the times has crept in through the cracks of the traditional fashion system. Fashion moves billions of dollars in the great capitals of the western world. Thanks to the 'just-in-time' formula, woman's universal and praiseworthy aspiration to look attractive is now attainable at reasonable cost to the majority. When Zara is accused of having brought nothing new to the world of fashion, the most accurate retort is that what it has really created is a new way to understand fashion and a different business model.

Fashion is the engine behind great financial empires; it creates thousands of jobs, buttressing the image of the country where it is designed. It has always been an accurate reflection of what is happening in society. We are all familiar with the comment by the French author, Anatole France, who said that if he were to return to earth a hundred years after his death, he would ask to look at a fashion magazine to get his bearings. He claimed that the dress styles and lifestyles shown in these publications are always the best indicators of what is current in society in any given age.

If we want to analyse what fashion means today we must take a look at what is happening in a wide range of fields – politics, economics, sociology – and fit them into the context of the globalisation in which we are living in this new millennium. This is the only way we can understand the emergence of a company of the size and characteristics presented by Zara, now comfortably established on five continents.

To an ever increasing extent, fashion is not just what we wear or following the latest trends, but everything that surrounds us. It is innovation and the direction we are moving in. Nowadays nothing is imposed upon us; rather, it is offered to us. We no longer turn our backs on the latest fashions; instead, we can allow ourselves to see them as something frivolous. Being taken over by the power that a trivial fashion has alerts us to the danger of rather silly ways of copying or adopting uniformity when we dress or how we live. We must strive to find our own identities, and individual creativity plays an important part in that process. We are legion, we women who wear Zara' basics to create an infinite mix of different looks by means of an accessory or a combination of unusual garments. The doorway is opening to fashion *a la carte*.

Enrique Loewe, an expert in the field, used to say in a course at the ISEM Fashion Business School that "fashion involves the luxury of looking at ourselves in the mirror and choosing the self we want to be, deciding on our own image. It is not a question of what we want to represent in life, but what we want to be, a clear display of authenticity. Faced with the thousand options we see on catwalks and in magazines, on the internet or television, the formula is not that of *having* many things, but rather that of *being* many things: being capable of building creative spaces where each individual finds his or her own personality, seeks new ideas, where we can bet on ourselves and transmit a personal aesthetic."

Is it be possible that this idea was one of the reasons why Amancio Ortega set out to lay the foundation stones of the company that has now taken over the world market, with store number 4,000 of the nine brands opened in September 2008 in Tokyo? Did the founder of Inditex have a hunch, soon to become a conviction, that a new culture of fashion was taking shape? His story, as we saw in the previous chapter, started in 1975 with the first Zara store in La Coruña. International expansion took place in the mid eighties. That was when the world was still under the influence of ostentation, led by the values of liberal capitalism and the values of the free market, when giant steps were taken towards pure, cold consumerism.

As Inmaculada Urrea states in her analysis of the 20th century[1*], "the cult of money became the theme of the decade, marked by post-

---

[1*] Desvistiendo el siglo xx [Undressing the 20th Century], Eiunsa, Madrid, 1999

modernism, design, hi-tech and yuppies who expressed a real obsession for image and appearances. Cynics, materialists and hedonists wanted to make money as quickly as possible so that they could enjoy an easy life of ostentatious luxury, favouring the resurgence of historical firms in the worlds of fashion as well as accessories." The decade saw the reappearance of Chanel under the hand of Karl Lagerfeld and Armani dressing executives with a look of timeless elegance. The catwalks were overwhelmed by luxury and the baroque. But these were also the years when perhaps in contrast, the concept of practical fashion emerged, with the aim of dressing the customer how she wanted to be dressed. That was the moment when Zara's clothing began to enjoy a warm welcome and to expand throughout the whole of Spain. By 1985, when expansion in our own country called for a more solid structure, Inditex had been set up to lead the group of companies.

"Being a businessman just to be rich is a waste of time."

Amancio is still on the job every day as he has been all his life, although now he arrives at Arteixo towards 11 in the morning rather than at nine o'clock as he used to. His clear-sightedness about the essence and future of the company way back when it was just a handful of people with no capital is a crucial factor in understanding the Inditex phenomenon. One of the company's top executives, Antonio Abril, who has been with the business since 1989, says that if you want an exact perception of this phenomenon, you have to see it through the eyes of the president. This opinion is shared by many in the factories, workshops and stores, not to mention the managers of the various brands with whom I spoke. Inditex cannot be understood without Amancio Ortega. I would go further; nothing of what has happened can be explained without this individual, the crucial pivot of the company that has moved thinkers, technicians, analysts and even the odd Nobel Laureate. What this visionary achieved is not just a string of technical successes due to strokes of genius and hours of hard work using his powerful brains, but something of a much greater scope.

The conclusion I reached after a long period of time attempting to understand Amancio Ortega and hearing the opinions and accounts of those who have known and worked with him is that every era produces geniuses of this kind. They are the ones who occupy a given position, such that after them, everything is different. I discussed this idea with Antonio Abril, a man with a wonderful reputation in the professional circles in which he moves, and he was forced to agree. Indeed, he added weight to my idea, saying that it held with such people as Leonardo da Vinci in art, Aristotle in metaphysics, Saint Thomas Aquinas in theology and Christopher Columbus who, while trying to find a route to Asia, instead, reached the Americas, leading to the first lasting European contact with the Americas and opening them for exploration and colonization.

Without having to press our explorations still further, we could even find in our own circle people such as Ramón Areces, founder of El Corte Inglés, the Spanish department store, or Tomás Pascual of the Spanish milk company, Grupo Leche Pascual, whom Ortega himself admires as a very special kind of businessman, never content to rest on his laurels. He always tried to go further, just as Amancio does, and for those reasons he and Pascual became good friends. His widow Pilar told me that on one occasion when they met, shortly before the death of her husband, he came back from America very impressed because Amancio told him that he could see his priorities in life very clearly. "Being a businessman just to be rich is a waste of time. When you make money the way we do, it's obvious that we shall never need more. For me, money has just one purpose. It's there so that you can achieve your goals. And if you're successful, then it's useful to help some of the many others who depend on us to make something of their lives." Pilar, no doubt a sincere admirer, added something else from the feminine point of view, "He may be unaware of what he achieved in addition to making money: the fact that a lot of people in no position to dress very well now feel rather less inferior in their everyday lives. Because thanks to Zara, being well dressed is within the reach of a large proportion of the population."

Along with this special gift that Amancio has – a mixture of intuition, natural intelligence, the ability to surround himself with people capable of carrying out his ideas plus never ceasing to work for a single day, another member of his team told me that God had granted him the physical and mental power to develop his company to a spectacular outcome, despite the fact that for many years its outline was seemingly atypical. When it started, there were no specific 'positions' at Inditex. Just as Amancio had no "table and chair" the people working with him knew what their duties were, but had no grand titles. His right-hand man in the company, professor of economics at La Coruña University, José María Castellano, was thrilled with the project. Since he began to work at Inditex he was responsible for the financial framework, later to develop into general management. Ortega's sister, Josefa, known as Pepita, who had worked at GOA was another of the pillars of the company, responsible for the liquid assets and an area that we would now call human resources. She was always the sweetest soul in the house.

From the very start of his adventure, Amancio had it clear that it was his mission to be the leader of the company; that meant that he would be directly responsible for commercial aspects that he found very exciting, and anyway, he could see this area with unusual clarity. This applied not only to the textiles side, but also to the real estate matter, and this was crucial to the development of the company. "I'm an architect *manqué*. I love plans and I read and interpret them with ease. I never have to leave a single element to being made up as I go along. From the initial project we were already shifting partitions and marking out spaces. It's in the shops that I really live, and the shops are Inditex's heart. I've poured myself into the creation of every one of them, from the first one in La Coruña, right up to those now being opened in Asia or the United Arab Emirates, although naturally I delegate more and more to the people in charge of the departments in question."

In actual fact, when it came to international expansion, he depended to a large extent on Fernando Martínez, who for years, he shared the job of seizing the best real estate with and who he made his international expansion chief. He is proud to travel through the world's capitals from Santiago in Chile to Stockholm via Dubai, Shanghai or Rio de Janeiro and find himself facing a magnificent building that displays the magic word Zara. The display windows reveal what is happening in these shopping areas that are almost always packed. Even when times are tough, they attract the public's attention with that special something printed on the displays and in the store interior. All of this is created by a group of artists who contentedly work on the ground floor in Arteixo alongside a passage where they set up the actual pilot stores. That's where they begin establishing the unmistakable style that is in every shop.

Amancio insists that he has delegated much of what were his duties at the start, and that is true; but the fact remains that his opinion – a word or even a gesture, can start off a small whirlwind. Everybody respects his point of view because that is what made them winners in every corner of the world. He is very conscious of this and he also knows that it is his responsibility to maintain the essence of the company. "Not long ago I was surprised to notice that in one of the pilot stores there was a corner which had a flavour that really didn't fit in with our shops. Straightaway I called over the person who was setting up the display window and pointed it out. I was concerned that he should see that it was actually a threat, not just to that specific store, but for Inditex as a whole, to display a look that didn't match our philosophy. It would be very counterproductive to start moving out of our market niche."

Ortega is still the one person who knows the ins and outs of the business to the smallest detail; someone always close by in the shadows, but with a powerful personality, a personality that does not overlook a single factor however trivial it may seem, and someone who perfectly blends firmness and toughness with a friendly and open approach, above all when it comes to listening to what his people say to him.

Ortega has also received extraordinary support from José María González Quintián, his personnel manager. He is one of the essential players whose faithful work Amancio has rewarded with suitable packages of shares, as he has with Fernando Martínez. These are good people with a clear philosophy: the quest for excellence. Amancio is genuinely obsessed by the idea of doing everything he touches as well as it can humanly be done. He is well aware of his limitations and shortcomings, what he can do and what he cannot do. He accepts the fact that it is impossible for him to know everything, so he is a force of nature in the fields where he is an expert. The way he works has one great advantage – it operates like a catapult to throw off the incompetent. At least, that is the conclusion I arrived at after talking with his people.

González Quintián knows the company and its president like the back of his hand. When I talked with him he insisted on the idea that you can only understand Inditex if you study the way Ortega operates, as his great strength, indeed, his great secret, is the way in which he steers the entire organisation. He uses a blend of authority and power with knowledge and passion. When I try to compare the opinions of those on his team with his own, Amancio's reply is more or less the same, "You have to allow people genuine independence. That's the key. And you have to stay close to the teams and make decisions along with them." It is of no importance that some of them will be more obvious because they occupy positions with a public face; he means the hundreds of employees at all levels who make up this huge team of professionals.

A few months ago, Inditex Human Resources manager for a short time, Jesús Vega, said in the magazine *Expansión* that when Ortega hired him, he gave him a word of advice for his job. He sums it up in one short sentence, "You have to like people." This very human focus contains one very profound part of his philosophy. The other part is to remain close, physically close, to his teams. Not a single person I talked to failed to highlight this facet.

You could categorically state that Amancio's workstation is the Arteixo building. To be more accurate, you could say it is the huge hall where the designers and commercial team are found. Here he spends endless hours working with the various sections, expressing his clear view and this basic idea, "In design, the world looks to Europe. European designers are young and have grown up in a global world. They have to be aware that clothing is universal because the customer is universal. We don't design clothes for 80 different countries; we design the same kind of clothing for 80 countries. That means that the product has to be exactly right. We're selling a fashion culture which overarches all the chains and the different brands." I heard him express this idea in just those words on more than one occasion. Only a few months ago he said it to a group of lecturers from business schools at a meeting at Inditex. It is his standard reply whenever someone asks him what the secret of his success is.

The rhythm of work is indefinable in a company that opens a new store every day. "Everything has to be done yesterday because tomorrow may be too late," I was told by Antonio Abril, a peaceful man, despite his weekly timetable of making at least five flights to different cities to solve problems that are as urgent as they are complex. The work of a general secretary like Antonio is basically legal, focusing mainly on store contracts, and it has grown at dizzying speed. "Ortega is keen to keep growing because he has proven that the product sells and as is natural, he has enormous ambition which is quite logical and healthy. He was unimpressed by outside meetings where little was decided in the end. He knew he was in control of the formula for success right now and he had no hesitation in putting it into practice at the same rapid rate as the market was following."

"Growth is a survival mechanism," Amancio once told me. That conviction is one of the engines that drive him.

Abril agreed that the way the factories and distribution centres are growing is also a mechanism. If there is no extra staff capacity, there is no flexibility. Ortega operates on the basis of a foundation that fills him with certainty in whatever he does. "We possess the formula, so we have to use it," he likes to say.

He is absolutely right. It is a fact that he never studied for any degree, he never took an MBA, but he has never been in any doubt as to the essence of his work. Everything he knows he taught himself and it has given him the conviction that he was always able to see the way the business worked. His trusted colleagues who have spent years with him admire him for this unique quality. When he talks of his first years heading up GOA, this is what he says about it, "When we started out with the famous quilted dressing gowns that everybody mentions, we used to sell to middlemen. In the end I was unsatisfied by that. We couldn't sell a pretty dress, however pretty it was, if what the customer was ordering at that precise moment was something else. I was convinced that I had to be in control of the customer and that I had to be close to the customer at the same time, but I could only manage that if I could sell directly to the customer. I was also convinced of something else if I was to carry out everything I had in mind: nobody buys on price alone. The first thing people want is to like what they want to buy. The product has to be right. That's the key."

This training, which he has never abandoned even during his moments of greatest success, means that Amancio always listens to his people, thanks them when they show him how he has made a mistake and how to set it right. On commercial matters, he repeats, "The one person who really knows this business is me."

Something that everybody who was with him at the birth of this great company wonders about is that during the early years – the tough years when there was little money about – he never saw money as a problem. "If it's true that I've made a lot of money, then it's because making money was never my goal," he told me some months ago. "I'll go further; in my opinion someone just out to make money is not much of a businessman."

As regards his favourite subjects, product and shops, of utmost importance for the business is Amancio's proactive style in making decisions. These are often risky decisions that the passage of time judges, such as opening in Mexico City. The decision was purely his and it turned out to become one of his greatest successes.

At the present time most of the premises are leased, as was mentioned earlier. "In the past I used to go in person so that I could see the city, the shop, the country. You must always go for the best, because the shop is the heart of the company; it's the protagonist in this company. There are places in the world where I've been determined to stay with a good spot that I've chosen, because however expensive it is, I can make it more profitable if it's in the right place."

As an example of his way of examining this aspect, I remember that in one of my chats with Antonio Abril, Inditex general secretary since 1989, he told me about a trip he made to Israel with Ortega to get to know this potential market. "He wanted to stroll about the streets, see what women were wearing there, how they lived. We spent three

days just soaking up the atmosphere. He wanted to
made every effort to be sure he was.

"Finally we devoted an entire day to visiting holy pl
had to see the emotion and acceptance Ortega expressed as ne kneeled
at the Holy Sepulchre. He has very deep beliefs. When we got back
to Santiago in the company plane, I went straight home and he went
straight to the factory because, as he put it, 'I've never gotten home
before 10 at night.' Nowadays he travels a lot less, but he's still aware
of what's happening even in the most faraway places. When one of
the staff, whether they're top brass or not, arrives from some new
city or country, they find themselves thoroughly questioned about
what's selling, why, how, and so on. Thanks to all this, Amancio is
able to say that 'the company was never like it is today. It's the nicest
company in the world.'"

To sum up the key to his success in just a few words, "You have to
increase coordination between the design area and the commercial
area. We are going to expand from 12,000 square metres to 24,000
for design. Nobody in the world would dare double that area."

When expansion turns into an explosion

In 1979, he brought all his companies together under the Inditex flag.
During the eighties he had taken his stores to every part of Spain, and
before the end of the decade he had the temerity to compete in the
fashion capitals of the world, opening up in Paris and crossing the
Atlantic to open shops in New York.

In the nineties, in step with the globalisation movement that was just
getting underway, his expansion became an explosion. Zara appeared
in the biggest cities in Europe, in the Far East and in a number of
Latin American capitals. Aware of the fact that a single brand would
never please every customer, Amancio decided not to rest with Zara,
which targets middle-class women and brings in 78 per cent of his
income. In 1991 he created Pull & Bear, supplying casual clothing
to the under twenty-fives. He also bought shares in Massimo Dutti,
which targeted customers of both sexes in the medium-to-high income

racket, and in five years he owned the brand completely. In 1998, with a view to meeting the needs of disco-frequenting teenagers, Bershka was born, with its hip-hop fun style for girls who don't want to dress like their mothers or elder sisters, and in the following year he bought Stradivarius to compete with Bershka, thus controlling two major brands in the teenage market.

Meanwhile, Amancio built up a team of top level executives around him, among whom the name of economist José María Castellano immediately catches the eye. Castellano came in as Vice-President of the company and worked at Ortega's side for 30 years. Also playing an important part was his nephew by marriage, Juan Carlos Rodríguez Cebrián, the husband of one of his sister Pepita's daughters, who held the position of managing director until a few years ago. With his help Ortega managed to run a stable of 99 companies with which complete vertical integration was assured, covering not just textiles and fabrication, but also logistics, marketing, construction, real estate, finance and power generation.

Inditex is the only one of the great companies in the clothing sector with a completely vertical organisation; the GAP and H&M design and sell, but don't manufacture, and Benetton designs and manufactures, but its points of sale are owned by franchisees. However, Ortega is the owner of almost all the properties acquired in the early years except for specific cases such as Germany and Japan, where a joint venture system is normally in place and some countries where for political or sociological reasons the franchise method works better. As time has passed and Inditex has grown, he has changed his formula for commercial premises and now they are usually leased.

Antonio Abril once told me that the Zara brand established itself as a phenomenon that cannot be defined from a purely economic point of view. Amancio Ortega created a business model that is studied in universities and academic institutions he had no chance to attend. Other golden rules comprise the structure vertical integration; rules that sustain the model and can be summed up in four basic points: flexibility of supply, instant absorption of market demand, response speed and technological innovation. According to José Luis Nueno, professor at the University of Navarra's IESE Business

School, Inditex overwhelmed the development models where six to nine months are needed to make a collection and are an echo of the times when brands held sway over consumers. "In nine months a lot can happen," says Nueno, "from changes in the weather that favour different colours or the appearance of Madonna in a lilac tee-shirt instead of a yellow one."

But the Galician textile model was conceived under the testing of setbacks. Its flexibility enables it to make last minute changes demanded by customers by means of the same production system that makes it possible to create a collection in four weeks and even in two, if that's what the market demands. "We have the ability to completely undo any production line if it isn't selling; we can dye the collections with new colours and we can create styles in just a few days." With this seemingly simple formula Amancio himself explains what we might dub the philosopher's stone of Zara's success.

In a study entitled "Zara, a challenge for mature thinking,"[2*] consultant Carlos Herreros de las Cuevas highlights the fact that contrary to the ideas of those who disagree with making big investments in the clothing manufacturing industry, a mature sector in which you milk the cow and make the best profit, the production process dreamt up by Ortega is capital and labour intensive. According to the author, the Zara phenomenon has shattered moulds and shown that mature businesses in which everything is in place do not exist, and that there are only companies or managers with closed minds who are resistant to innovation.

Inditex possesses the latest generation of technology, and although that implies a higher labour cost, it means that in the early years they were able to produce over 50 per cent of their collections in their own factories and in Spanish and Portuguese cooperatives. The rest was outsourced to the Maghreb and the Far East under clearly defined guidelines. The units of the ultramodern premises in Galicia are connected by over 200 kilometres of underground access routes to a fully-automated logistics centre located in Arteixo. From here,

---

[2*] HFC Consultores, S.L., 30 December 2002.

loaded lorries leave for shops in Europe or for airplanes to the rest of the world. This process, combining information in real time and actual production with an efficient distribution system, means that it is possible to operate with zero stock and avoid having to sell off surpluses, thus generating an added value that in the final analysis, balances out costs.

The marketing strategy included innovations such as "re-educating" the customer. Traditionally the vendor made sure of high margins at the start of the season, but then tolerated several months of reductions to get rid of stock. The customer knows that in the end she can buy the same garments at lower prices. The Ortega business renews its garments in its shops worldwide every week and twice a week in its European stores. Customers know that they will always find new items, but also that they will definitely not find whatever it was they tried on seven days ago. This means that if customers see something they like, they must buy it straightaway, because in a few days it will be nowhere to be found in the store. "The aim is to create a climate of scarcity and opportunity," explains Luis Blanc, a former executive for the company for which he expresses deep admiration. This environment resulted in the fact that, in Spain, consumers visit an Inditex store 17 times per year on average as opposed to the 3.5 visits recorded for other fashion chains.

The key to the success of a groundbreaking company

So what is the key to the success of a company? I would like to encourage anyone keen on understanding this phenomenon to take a look around the headquarters of Planet Zara one of these days. Visits are non-stop and the staff whose job it is to explain how the Arteixo plant works, pay 100 per cent attention to the clients. That is how to take the pulse of the company.

It is 11 o'clock in the morning in the Sabón industrial zone (in La Coruña) where, Inditex has its general headquarters that cover an area equal in size to 47 football fields, not to mention 30,000 square metres of new buildings. The president's car has just driven through the security barrier of the new 'intelligent building', just finished at a cost of 1,500 million pesetas. (nine million euros) "Here he is," they are thinking in the Zara Woman section, where the president usually spends his working day if he is not travelling. The footfalls of Amancio Ortega echo along the austere, functional passageways that are devoid of anything that would count as a distraction from work. You would be surprised to find out how high the percentage is of self-made men and women who have risen to the top of this business. For example, an ex-lorry-driver is currently the highest authority on men's shirts. Even so, the company's unstoppable growth has destroyed something of the familiarity that once characterised this company with its multinational face and paternalistic style. Amancio has also given up his habit of making it a point to visit Torreiro on Saturdays, the Zara closest to his home that faces the sea, and the most iconic store of all in La Coruña.

The employees who know him best and have the most to do with him highlight his intuition, creativity, ability to delegate and encourage every individual to accept responsibility for their own work, his total dedication to the company, democratic principles and his ability to listen. On the negative side, they point to his unlimited ambition that does not express itself as personal vanity, but takes the form of an obsession to raise up his company at all costs to the top position on the podium. They also mention his pigheadedness and his habit of encouraging competition within the team. But when forced to pick out one aspect of his character, it is his aversion to the term "exclusivity". He would never allow his designers and commercial people to place their personal interests before those of the company. He makes them feel obliged to share all the discoveries they have made during his trips to London, Tokyo, New York or India with his team, just as he has done all his life. Commercial egotism, so much a feature of luxury brands, has been exiled from the premises at Sabón.

Those who know him insist that Amancio Ortega likes to get his own way. If the experts are against opening a Zara in Venezuela and he is convinced that there has to be one there, he will buy the most expensive building he has so far purchased in the history of the company (8,000 million pesetas; 48 million euros). For those stud the Inditex phenomenon from the business angle, its president represents the classic type of self-made businessman, like Rothschild or Rockefeller, who builds his power on a foundation of talent and effort. This ordinary man has brought a democratic view never seen before in this area to the culture of fashion.

Ortega has devoted his life to a struggle against appearances in which no quarter is given. His life is the company and his philosophy is well known: in the early days money was the means he used to advance the company; everything he earned was invested in it. Nowadays his focus is more on maintaining the families that depend on Inditex for their jobs. What Ortega really seeks is to not find himself halfway on the road to excellence. He must be satisfied.

He is unostentatious in his tastes and in the way he dresses or eats. He is irked by show, and this has become a fundamental aspect of the success of Inditex. Some years ago (the narrator laughed when he told me, as he felt involved in the story), someone on the management team bought a Porsche while somebody else had bought a very basic fishing boat. At a work meeting, in order not to make the former employee in whom he had less confidence feel uncomfortable, he said to the latter member in such a way that everybody listening would understand, "I wonder if you'll end up having to sell the boat, because it looks as though we might be being squeezed out of the luxury trade!" Ortega, of course, owns a very beautiful yacht, the *Valoria*, in which he loves to explore the Rías Bajas (rivers in the southern part of La Coruña), but it is still not the boat that one of the richest men in Spain would have bought. He aims to be at peace with his family, pursuing the same lifestyle as before.

By way of conclusion, in the actual words of a worker who knows Amancio well, "He's someone with a great deal of personal charm because he's genuine. There's no side to him. He is capable of being tough, impulsive and very sure of himself, but what you see is always what you get." This particular man concluded his memories by telling me that "after he floated the company, when his photograph was distributed in the press, there was one particular afternoon when he had gone to the airport to collect his wife who was on her way back from a trip. He was recognised, and he felt so embarrassed that he had to wait for her in the car."

The Inditex president blends the great confidence that he has in his people with ambition for the business. This is a challenging strategy that he defines like this, "We built a garage, and almost immediately we were wondering why we didn't add two more floors."

There is no room for doubt that in this new fashion culture of the 21st century, an individual like Ortega has all the cards that he needs in his hand to win the game.

4

Ortega Always Pursued Excellence

Not everything that happened in his life and in the life of Inditex can be told by Amancio himself. In his long career of over 60 years there is a great deal of information including many situations that can be explained in greater detail from a very personal standpoint. Instead, this is explained by the people who have shared and walked his entrepreneurial journey step by step. All the people I talked with about Amancio Ortega accept the undeniable fact that the Inditex reality merges with the story of the founder. Until recently, on the grounds of absolute loyalty and the almost reverential respect for the position their president has always maintained, they have revealed no details about his private life; nobody had come forward to talk.

Everything changed the day that Amancio, having expressed his trust in me and his invaluable friendship, agreed not only to my telling some part of our conversations in this book, but allowed me to carry out a certain amount of research based on questions and conversations with the members of his team. They would add more information and direct knowledge to my perception of this story and his life. He wisely advised me not to produce a rose-coloured spectacles view, and counselled that I should seek other sources of information, "as long as they are objective, for better or worse," all backed by plain common sense. For example, he suggested that I might be wasting my time talking to his sister Pepita, "Because, my dear, Pepita adores me. As far as she's concerned, I'm the tops. What can she tell you in addition to that? No, you'll do better to talk to people who won't be quite so wholehearted. Best to leave out the family sources!" Since my main purpose is that everybody – readers, Amancio's family and the man himself, can sample these pages that I hope will be objective, I took his advice and abandoned my interviews with his older sister Pepita, who was with him in the first years of his adventure, for another occasion.

Amancio insisted that I seek an impartial approach to describe him or anybody else. "You can't expect me to be talking to you hour after hour about myself and what I've done. You know that would be ridiculous. You should get others to tell you what they know best, because they will have done it along with me. And please, not just the good things or just the bad things. Get them to tell you the truth, the things that they believe they can explain to you. You will find that everybody explains things from their own point of view. Nobody will tell you the identical story because we all see things in our own way. And you'll realise that Inditex is the story of many thousands of people who've left their mark on the company." That was his way of saying that he was now keeping his nose out; it was up to me to write the book and to try not to fall for extremes.

In quite an unexpected way, once he had given his approval to my project and let his people know that if they wished, they were free to talk to me without any restrictions, it turned out to be quite easy to go to the most direct sources in search of information and anecdotes that would illuminate the way I saw things myself. From then on, I just talked to people from all levels of the company, trying to get the most balanced picture of how the empire had come to be built. As he suggested, I also talked with a number of people who had spent greater or lesser periods of time at his side and who, for various reasons, were no longer at Inditex. It was certainly not my intention to seek out nothing but high praise for the president; rather, I wanted the true opinion of those who had accompanied him through the ups and downs that are unavoidable in any project that results from human hands.

"I intend to make what the customers want."

Diego Copado, a fine professional who was communications manager for the company for over eight years told me that Amancio was still very young when he became an La Coruña textile manufacturer selling his product to everyone who had a shop in Spain at the time. He bought fabric, manufactured and sold his production as a wholesaler to retailers or to the shops themselves. He did this until he realised that the system had to change, since the customer, because of the competition which was beginning to build, was going to end up with many more options to choose from.

"I'm going to manufacture what I understand the customers are going to demand," he said to himself. That decision, borne yet again from that intuition that surprises everybody who knows Amancio, was the seed of today's business group. Year later, Copado explained to me that the central idea of the success of Inditex is that at any given moment Ortega intuits, understands and sets off on a course that he sees as necessary; that the customer is going to be given power that she has hitherto not had. While at first, customers may have been won over on price with new and attractive products yet without a clear vision of what was being sold – Amancio himself realised that there was no way of knowing where this policy would end up – Amancio was a visionary when the moment came to apply a model linked to the customer's desires. At first, he was one step behind this: let's manufacture along the lines of what's happening; if the market wants this, let's do it. And so he built up his business by trying to get to know and to listen to the consumer.

In 1975 he adapted his entire project to this view of the future and became fully involved in the field of distribution, unaware that in the USA, a company called the GAP existed. Spain was a very different country then, unlike today when its communications use all available media at the global level. Mass retail in Spain was unknown in those years when Ortega was rooted in the northwest of the Iberian peninsula. Company legend has it that the mainstay of the business ran along National Highway 6 that then linked La Coruña with Madrid, as well as with some small businesses in Galicia.

When they reached Madrid they opened a small shop. It was an intelligent way to grow, and they continued to consolidate the model, little by little, with small teams and always on the *qui vive* to pick up any hints that might improve the company. To Amancio's tireless mind it was clear that if he wanted to be a leader in the sector in the 20th century, the next step was to computerise the company. He rapidly realised how essential it was to share his project with professionals who had the experience and desire to become completely involved in technical areas such as management. It was at that moment that he took one of the most important steps in his career by taking on someone who was not part of the family circle.

José María Castellano:
"What Ortega has done can never be repeated."

Taking on José María Castellano was crucial for the development of Inditex. Castellano began as an external consultant while still with GOA until the time came when Ortega realised that the company needed a general manager with a strong commitment to the project. The result was a very effective union of one man with a financial and corporate background, able to direct the company from all aspects, with someone who had unerring commercial sense. As time passed, other professionals in various fields were added to the company, but the basics were already in place.

Ortega always liked the simplest ideas; he preferred to clarify problems and decisions to be made in the most direct and speedy way possible. He is not given to lengthy technical expositions. "What are they good for?" is his usual question. He prefers the pragmatic approach, another quality which has doubtless been of great importance to him. Castellano was also able to focus on problems from this point of view, the outcome being that they were able to build a team that produced excellent results.

"Caste," as he is known by both friends and everyone who has worked with him, has been Ortega's right-hand man for 30 years. Everyone I asked agreed that he is a unique professional, a man of integrity, sound, hard-working, unremitting and someone who joined Inditex at a crucial moment to become CEO and Vice-President for 20 years.

I have had the good fortune to meet and talk with him on various occasions. We shared meals with Amancio Ortega and he also taught at the ISEM Fashion Business School, giving some excellent sessions not only on financial subjects, but also dealing with humanities. I remember the way the students listened to him; they all wanted to know more about him, to get him to come up with more personal responses, which always left them smiling. He even gave them his card so that they would be able to become thoroughly versed in the business model he was explaining to them. After those classes several of the students made their way to the northeast of Spain to work with Inditex.

It goes without saying that José María Castellano knew how keen I was to write this book. Every time we met he would ask me how it was going and give me a look that consisted of a mixture of scepticism and irony when I told him that it wasn't easy, but that I was sure in the end I would finish it. Because he had that way of supporting good projects from the wings, I knew I had his support in persuading Ortega to give me definite approval and that he would ensure that his boss saw things in the right light. Sometime later, when I called to tell him that I now had authorisation to tell the true story of the engine behind Inditex, he was absolutely delighted. By that time José María had left the company and all the gossip that surrounded his departure was now left in the past. With complete confidence I told him that I felt it was essential to get his opinion about Amancio, connected though it might be with that final, unexpected and controversial event that caused him to leave the company that he had worked so hard for with such remarkable results. I made it quite clear that I had no wish to pry into matters that might embarrass him or cause pain, but I also explained that a book about Ortega and Inditex without a contribution from one of the most important protagonists would obviously lack any credibility.

His reply was immediate. He would be delighted to talk with me and he congratulated me on the conquest of that fortress that had seemed impenetrable. "What happened, happened, and I'm really not interested in talking about it," were his words regarding his departure. I fully shared his point of view, so we arranged to meet for him to tell me his memories and give his opinion about Inditex and Amancio. Everything worked out very positively. For a full two hours he told me about his experience, which I felt was very valuable and pivotal to an understanding of the reality of this business trajectory that really was out of the ordinary.

"A Zara culture does exist. What Ortega has done could never be repeated in the same way. He is a person with an intuitive appreciation and vision of the future that history grants to very few. He has been able to motivate a large number of people to devote themselves to the project unconditionally. It may have turned out badly for some, but that's life. When a course has been set for a business there will always be someone who doesn't understand it, or who disagrees with it, or who simply can't accept the company goals as his own. That happens in any situation, be it human, political, social, whatever. But I always maintain that fortunately, this company left few casualties behind, and that is a good thing.

"I joined the company in 1974. There was nothing complicated about it. I met Ortega when only the factories with which he worked existed; Zara did not exist. At that time nobody thought about technology in our sector – computers and the like were non-existent in the area – and he was keen to have a good team from this point of view. It was another example of his focus on the future. It happened that I'd worked on a scholarship at IBM and also with an insurance company, Aegon, where I was the data processing manager. We'd brought in System 3, which was very modern at that time, and so when Ortega got in touch with me with the idea of taking somebody else on, I organised the data processing team. We set him up with a system which at that time, despite the fact it was the best you could get, was very primitive, just as you would have found anywhere else in the world at that time. But that was the embryo of what was to become of the group.

"Ortega wanted me to stay with him but I was teaching economics at the university at the time, and was about to go for a professorship, so I turned him down. But the person who worked with me stayed and set up the system with him. I continued as a consultant, not just for data processing, but also in areas linking the organisation and the thousand things that were coming up at that time, until in the end I did join the company in 1984. By that time the group had four factories: GOA, Sanlor, Fíos and Noite, and 24 shops. Inditex didn't exist as a company until 1988.

"And it's at this point that another stage began that was very important for the future of the company. When Ortega went to El Corte Inglés to sell his products, the buyers were asking for the kind of products that when they hit the street were clearly not what the customers wanted. That was why he started to think about having his own shops. There was nothing special about the first one he opened and above all, it had nothing to do with the current concept of the Zara shops. But fairly soon, they started to change things with a focus on that idea of fast production that has been the success of the business. Initially everything was done in the factories the group owned, but as Zara grew, they started to outsource to workshops all over Galicia. Cutting was always done in the factories and the patterns were sent out to the workshops. Lots of them weren't even workshops, they were just groups of women in flats – someone sewed the sleeves, someone sewed on the buttons and someone else did the buttonholes.

"The nub of the question was whether Ortega, who used to sell in a shop, would allow himself to be guided by an intuition that was showing him how you ought to operate in this sector, and indeed, he took that path. But it's one thing to have the idea of a shop and quite another to apply that same idea to three thousand shops in over 69 countries and to set up eight chains, which is what we subsequently did, with everybody following that motivational idea of his."

As if guessing what I was thinking, and the natural next question of how he had managed to achieve it, he explains that one of the secrets of success is that Amancio is usually open to suggestions from anyone who knows more than he does in areas where he feels he is no expert. "Ortega listens to everybody and soaks it all up like a sponge, absorbing what fashion trend makers think and the opinions of the movers and shakers in the field. Knowing how a business works means more than the sum total of degrees and MBAs studied.

The Inditex philosophy has been founded on listening to what's happening in the world and that's why it has been so fantastically successful. It's not just that Ortega knows how to listen, but that he always gave a great amount of responsibility to the people in touch with the customers. His ability to synthesise the most complex ideas as though they were really simple is an extraordinary quality, and it is something he has done all his life."

I take the opportunity to ask José María Castellano what he thinks is the kernel of the business. "There's no doubt that the shop is a basic factor that Ortega always saw in an unequivocal way. Staying close to the customer was a great advantage over those who failed to notice change. At that time, fashion focused on presenting two very established traditional collections per year. Nobody was interested in the street. Designers had no idea what customers thought about their collections, and it was this approach to focusing fashion that Inditex turned upside down. Of course, there's no doubt that you can do this for a single shop, as I've said. The problem arises when you want to grow and repeat this business model. The result is an organisational problem; the problem of moving from ideology to technology. It was a real challenge to seek out and build up teams who could implement not just the idea, the philosophy, but who could handle the organisation and control it at the worldwide level while the business model kept growing.

"Ortega never slacked in the pursuit of excellence; he always thought that the company came first, and everybody else next. I feel it was a very positive starting point; the company was taken care of in the sense that he invested all the money in it that it needed and what was left over was invested in dividends. The workers realised that he believed in them and in the company, and to help it grow they gave everything they could."

When I asked him about worker loyalty, he told me that Inditex is "a company of young people and a great deal has been delegated to them as far as responsibility is concerned. They are allowed to make decisions. If, for example, a store manager talks to someone from the marketing side, that's because marketing personnel have the power to make decisions. In other companies in the sector the people who decide are usually the buyers. Here, the people who decide are salespeople with decision-making powers. In other words, people who aren't bound by budgetary control. What you don't find here is the order, 'You have to buy 50,000 metres of denim', because if this season's fashion isn't jeans, you don't buy it. There's no financial team giving orders to a commercial team; the people who get preference in decision-making are the people who are in contact with the customers. This is a large part of the secret of the company and it explains a lot of what has happened in the company. Ortega starts from there, from a shop, and never claims to tell the customers what they must buy."

Naturally, I would like this conversation to reveal which roles were played by Castellano and Ortega in big company decisions. The explanation could not have been more direct or straightforward. "Things were negotiated in the various departments and when a decision was reached, it went to Ortega to decide on the best strategy. Once the course to follow had been approved, Ortega delegated responsibilities to various people with absolute trust to put those decisions into effect. Matters were put on the table to be studied and decided upon, not to be imposed on people. I remember the time when the owner of the company Sephora was keen to sell it to us, but then it ended up with the LVMH group. Ortega and I were in complete agreement over the fact that it was important to buy it, but the rest of the company didn't see it like that. We thought it could be effective to combine clothes with something else, but the majority felt that this would be a distraction and that we had to keep investing in Zara. They thought that cosmetics and perfumes were businesses we neither knew about nor could manage. The end result was that we didn't buy the company. This is what I would call a form of 'intelligent flexibility' when it comes to running a big business that is growing quickly.

"International expansion decisions were also important. The United States, for example, is not the strong point for Zara and the other chains; we never intended it to be. It was a very carefully worked out managerial decision. On the one hand, at that time the US currency was very strong, and on top of that, except in the big cities, American customers were used to very basic products from places like the GAP.

They didn't share the same interest in fashion as in other countries. We were convinced that we still had a great deal to do in Europe, and we settled on the idea of opening a flagship store in New York, as much for brand image, and then to open three or four stores per year in the US, while in Europe we would be opening 400. Zara was part of a European company. We had begun with Portugal in 1988, in a market where there was hardly any competition; no other chains existed and we could see big growth possibilities. From France we went to Belgium, the Netherlands, Greece, etc. Amancio dislikes flying and in those days he would travel thousands of miles by car or train. He was changing his car every year. Despite the fact that he owns his own private plane, he has never been keen on flying, except for when he has to do it for obvious reasons like crossing the Atlantic, for example, or avoiding excessively long land journeys when too much time is wasted."

I continue to express my curiosity about the division of labour between Castellano and Ortega. "Was it very carefully worked out?" I asked. "To the contrary, it worked out quite naturally. Amancio was always very drawn to the commercial area, where in those days he had around 200 increasingly international designers covering the entire world in search of the latest trends and what the customers really wanted. Today there are 600, which meant that at his side, I could get on with my own field."

I take the opportunity to ask Castellano about a matter which I mentioned in the opening pages of this book – the talks they had with Armani. "Armani's company was up for sale, and he offered it to Inditex. We had several conversations, but it all came to nothing in the end because all they were selling was the business, not the name, and the product without the brand name has no meaning. We met on several occasions and both parties came to understand that this kind of a formula could sink us both. The more the talks went on with management, the more impossible their offer appeared. Now they're making their way with a big family empire and their future is in the balance. It was also common knowledge that there was an offer on the table from Loewe, the great Spanish luxury brand with a fantastic tradition and enormous possibilities, but it kept going around the houses too much. Now they have an excellent CEO, Albert Puyol, and they form part of the LVMH holding. We could not leave the brand image in the hands of a third party, however high that third party might have been placed in world rankings of luxury goods.

"There have always been companies that wanted to sell and that have approached Ortega, but a luxury company strategy is different from that of a retailer. You have to remain very balanced and keep your goals very clear in order not to stray from your own line of business. That doesn't mean that you don't set out every day to do better, but you mustn't lose contact with your own company's DNA. One of Amancio's great objectives was to fix it so that the whole world could dress well. So why get involved in businesses that weren't yours? Keeping a cool head, applying maximum standards and seeking ambitious goals always kept us in our own field."

I remark to José María Castellano that from the outside, it appears they never felt they were better than anybody else, and that they always accepted the success of others. "All I can say is that I saw myself as a very lucky man. Luck is important in everything you do in this life along with factors such as talent, work and so on. Anybody who doesn't believe in luck should watch the film *Match Point*. Amancio never believed he was the only one. He's humble, intelligent, hard-working and never wanted to rise beyond his circle of friends. We never sought the limelight, either personally or as a company. And it's more complicated to maintain a position of balance, rejecting ostentation, in a small city than it is in a big one. In Madrid, for example, a company like Inditex is diluted because there are so many others of the same size, while in a little city you can't help seeing yourself as the general giving orders in the parade ground because there are so few of you in the same situation. You can end up thinking that you're the king of the world, and you really aren't. Thanks to the fact that we've had to move around and travel a great deal, we've managed to remain normal, rather than becoming aliens in our hometown."

As regards the future of Inditex, the former CEO is of the opinion that, "the company float was undertaken from the point of view that this is a strong group established for the time when Ortega can no longer control the day-to-day activities. It was positive: the governance of the company was improved; a form of discipline was imposed within given guidelines. No, I'm not worried about the future. From the family angle I imagine that Ortega's daughter will take over as head, while he will carry on as the figurehead because he's the kind of man who dies with his boots on. The company is his life."

I was intrigued to find out the genesis of the situations that have become case studies in business schools at an international level. For Castellano, "the explanation is obvious. I thought because of the policy that has been followed up to now, that when we floated the company we were about to become completely unknown. The case studies offered ways that potential investors could get to know who we were. The Harvard case, for example, was bought by two million people. Wal-Mart used to hold the record with one million. This helped us a great deal to become known in the business world."

When I ask him why there is only one other brand with the same name, Zara Home, he tells me that, "taking care of the Zara name was crucial. If your most important brand, the one the company depends on, is burdened with an extra word, and you launch a brand that fails, it would become a disaster and drag the main name down with it, apart from the fact that it isn't a good idea to repeat a name too often."

I remark that many incorrect stories have been told about Inditex, as with other companies, such as the one about the way it exploited its workers. According to Castellano, "there are too many people who talk for the sake of talking. At about that time, Fraga (Manuel Fraga, Galician politician, father of the 1978 Spanish constitution and founder of the Popular Party) once rang me up and said, 'I've just been talking to Jordi Pujol (another Galician politician) and he wondered what connection there was between Zara and drugs'. I recall that it was a typical Galician Saturday, raining cats and dogs. I said, 'I'm going to ask you to do something for me. Ring Mr Pujol and tell him that Ortega and I would like to talk to him.' He called him and the pair of us paid a visit. Pujol then made a second mistake, because he mixed us up. 'You talk,' Ortega told me at the start, and the Honourable Member of the Catalan Parliament thought that I was the boss. The famous photograph of Ortega had not yet been publicised. We explained the situation.

It's a sad fact that when a company grows big and is successful, nobody is interested in the truth about it, which is that it has succeeded because everybody has worked hard and well. It's easy to invent stories and spin all kinds of yarns about drugs, about ships on the high seas, etc. As for exploiting the workers, it was just another of the baseless rumours that circulate about winners. Nobody ever did anything except work at Inditex. A lot of people learned a great deal, a lot of people found a lot of opportunities. The company took chances by investing in itself, because we believed in what we were doing and we worked with intelligence, effort and sobriety. The owners lived like any other modest family because they didn't invest in luxuries."

Castellano still thinks that Zara ought to open a school to teach people in the field. The system he invented is impressive, but it has to develop. His conclusion is, "You never get anything from Amancio that isn't positive. After working together for 31 years, I still maintain that the trust he placed in me was absolute. He helped me to understand a number of important things including the fact that intelligence is what helps you appreciate beauty. I wish him nothing but the best."

"Amancio is a good business manager."

A few days later, I picked up my conversation again with Diego Copado, Communications Manager. He's with a company whose most representative brand, Zara, boasts only a single page of advertising in an age of sales. He no longer works with the company but he knows Ortega well, and is thus able to analyse him with perspective and objectivity.

"Amancio is a good business manager, a very intuitive person and very open to those around him. He has a very clear idea of what he wants, not because he's always out there getting to know about what's happening on the street but because he's very aware of what the company thinks and is surrounded by young people who are very much involved in social change. Ortega is very observant, listens as a matter of course and in a premeditated way. This is a great quality.

He isn't the kind of man who is afraid of losing impetus by endlessly growing; he never feels caught off-guard. He's very aware of the fact that a business like distribution, particularly in fashion, has to be connected with what's happening. The lasting memory I have is of somebody who is accessible while being the president of the company."

I had always wanted to know what most attracts Ortega's attention when it comes to hiring new people, and Copado says, "He has that philosophy that you should never anchor people in the same spot. In all sections there is a lot of rotation, because he sees it as very positive. He's always open to what's new, to growing by taking on new values, by taking account of what young people tell him – people between the ages of 20 and 30. Commercially, he always wants restless personalities, people who question things and see beyond the obvious; people who launch new initiatives. One of Inditex's values is just that, about the ability to act outside of the box."

As far as the business model is concerned, Copado believes that "he invented nothing. Ortega has been an observer who rejects all straitjackets. My job was to sell in a company that at the beginning of 1988 was not the great company we know today. It was more like a small family business. Fashion was very different in those days. Everything happened in six countries and while the international aspect was at a stage where some progress had been made, we still had a long way to go before we could turn ourselves into an international company. We had to create a brand at the retail level, and the horizon where we could float the company was still far in the distance. These were matters with set times that had to be dealt with very seriously."

It seems that Ortega was not very keen on the idea of quoting the company on the stock exchange. The basic idea you get from those who were close to him at that stage is that this was a step that really made him hesitate. Ortega is a businessman, a shopkeeper, a man who knows his products. He likes order and being a quoted company forces you to follow very strict plans. In itself, he would find it an excellent idea; what he didn't like was the fact that he would be dependent on external opinions and that really had him weighing up the pros and cons.

There were a number of matters which needed clarification on top of the day-to-day ups and downs, and they included the succession and future of the group. Certain peculiarities existed in terms of the structure of the capital, involving his ex-wife and the key shareholders, who were almost all members of his family. Floating the company meant that other ways of funding the future of the company would be found and the project had to be protected. If things were done well, it would safeguard the company to introduce a higher level of professionalism. When it was possible to see this in hindsight, it was clear that everything had indeed been very soundly constructed.

"At that time Ortega was completely unknown. 'Did he exist or not?' asked the media, including the financial press. Hidden paparazzi lurked undercover in the environs of Arteixo trying to reveal this anonymous man. In those days the communications department did not exist. From time to time, people attempted to perform those kinds of duties, but they barely lasted a few months. A journalist acted as spokesperson without any clear idea of his future in the company. Someone recommended that Ortega upgrade the level of professionalism in this area and my name was put forward. At the time I was working as a consultant. 'We need someone because I know nothing about communications. So from here on, you're it.' That was how I was hired. And that was how interest began to grow in Ortega and in Zara. Inditex was yet to come into existence."

Copado says that Ortega didn't like filling his agenda with things that didn't matter. Since he believes in teamwork and believes that the best kind of communication is in the things the company does, he understood that a distribution company needed to communicate its image and its product. He was very aware of the fact that things were going to be different when the company was quoted on the stock exchange.

"Ortega doesn't like to be in the public eye, which is why he very carefully weighs up what is essential for him as a manager and what might restrict his private life. When the time came, he agreed to his picture being publicised so that he wouldn't be an anonymous, faceless character. In that way we at least partly did away with the story of the man who was never seen, about whom various dark

The Man from Zara

legends were associated. But the fact is that if somebody prefers not to have a public presence, that wish has to be respected."

When it comes to business projects, Copado points to Ortega's clear perception of the way society behaves and picking up on the fact that people were beginning to call for a greater degree of freedom and transfer their demands to the distributors. He was also able to foresee which kinds of skills would come into being that did not yet exist. "The idea that 'people don't do that' was never an argument that carried any weight with Ortega. 'People may not do that, but I intend to,' he would reply. At that time the company was a very free organisation, with a very open mind. The fact that the company was located on the edge of things was also very helpful, because it was free of the restrictions found in big capitals. It suited them very well because they felt none of the tension of being installed in an entrepreneurial environment; the business was not subject to the same pressures as one in Madrid or Barcelona. They weren't rubbing shoulders on a daily basis with consultants, advertisers, analysts and the like and they made the most of that situation.

"Initially it was a family business that when you saw it close up, you sensed it consisted of a successful team; people with an unusual style, with a great deal of transparency. It was very motivational seeing the way they worked, as was the responsibility they gave you. They were daring. They had no set frameworks."

The next thing I ask the former communications manager is whether, in his opinion, Amancio is highly gifted. "A highly gifted person who has continued to educate himself – which has the double interpretation of any professional. If you devote 90 per cent to what you do, you are bound to find that other facets of your life also benefit. On the entrepreneurial level, Ortega is highly gifted in the distribution field, the field which he has devoted 99 per cent of himself to, but that can give rise to a lot of handicaps in other fields. Everything depends on where you channel your passion. The area of distribution has been much enriched by Ortega's passion because he created a model that contributed a great deal to society and gave the sector a lot to think about. If Ortega were to place more emphasis on other aspects and if he had not devoted himself to Inditex in the way he has, then he would simply not be the person he is. He absorbs the goodness that he finds in his environment and builds everything he possibly can into his life. I repeat the fact that he brings passion to what interests him, and you must consider what that means when you work with someone with such a strong personality. That passion makes him see the world in a different way from everybody else."

A genius with the mind of a shop assistant

Antonio Camuñas, former president of the Spanish Chamber of Commerce in New York, played a very important part in the life of Amancio Ortega at the time that Inditex was being floated. That was the time when the company was growing at a dramatic rate, and Ortega's obsession with remaining anonymous and not appearing in public was giving rise to all kinds of rumours that could have damaged his empire. What Camuñas did was important, of that there is no doubt, and for that reason I asked him to explain it to me personally.

It wasn't easy to track down this businessman who spends half his life in an aeroplane and the rest in Manhattan and Madrid, but he managed to create a window and welcomed me into his office. With great acuity and deep admiration for the protagonist of this book, he gave free rein to his memories. He provided me with a very clear and eloquent summary of those days. "The job was to introduce outstanding personalities from the financial, political, economic or social worlds to the company, and to organise the key action and to have a face-to-face meal with the founder and president. For a period of 10 years or so, these visits were organised once or twice a month." The widest range of people, from Felipe González (ex-president of Spain, 1982–1996) to Emilio Botín (chairman of Santander Central Hispano bank) or Antonio Garrigues (chairman of Garrigues, one of Spain's biggest law firms), left those meetings with the same impression – Ortega is a very approachable man, and reserved, while possessing an absolutely unique talent for surrounding himself with extraordinary people.

With just a few words, Camuñas provided me with a picture of the exchanges and opinions aired at several of those fascinating dinners at which a myriad of different subjects were tackled. It was never in any doubt that Ortega is a person with a level of natural intelligence quite out of the normal range and that he enjoyed genius-level insight. This led him to transform his tiny company from what it was in the seventies into the huge textile distribution company we know today. 'How did it happen?' he asked himself in our conversation. And he provided his own reply, "For me the key is that he has the mentality of a shop assistant. Having observed him throughout all these years, my conclusion is that he has developed an extraordinary sensitivity for what people want. And the only person who can do that is someone who cut their teeth working in a shop. Obviously, the personality of the owner is very different from that of the person who does the selling, because the owner has the things that he, the owner, likes. This is an important shade of difference when it comes to grasping the character of this genius. And the shop assistant, who has had no part in the process of choosing what he likes, has just one goal: to sell.

"In my opinion, this is how you can sum up his story. Initially, he had nothing to say about what was purchased or what the shop stocked; the only task he had was to work out what people liked. That was his school: observing and learning by noticing the changes in the tastes and preferences of the public; what women liked best, what pleased girls or young boys or indeed anybody who came in. In this sense, Inditex is a company based on reality. At the opening of each season, Zara launches a first collection of trends, and from that moment on it is watching what the customers want, and continues manufacturing that line since that's what the market wants. Day after day information is analysed so that the public can be supplied with what they want. Ortega is at the forefront of the customer service field. What looks incredibly simple is nothing less than a revolution; realising that the customer has expectations that should not be thwarted, striving to supply the customer with a response and demonstrating an ability to do so."

5

Inditex – International Expansion

Paris, 1990

One April day a few years ago, I went to La Coruña to organise a visit to Inditex for a group of MBA students from the ISEM Fashion Business School. As always, when I have the opportunity to do so, I made a point of saying hello to Amancio who happened to be in Arteixo, and I made a point of mentioning the fantastic contribution he had made – indirect but fundamental – when the first steps were being taken in this educational project.

In 2001, when the ISEM Fashion Business School was just about to be launched, Ortega gave me two pieces of advice, and they were fundamental: we should aim for excellence from day one and we should think very carefully about where we would locate the school. "It has to be in Madrid or Barcelona. I'm the only person who has any idea how hard it is to drag good professionals out to Finisterre. Of course, I'm well aware that this part of the world is special and people from this region give you all they've got. But getting here, and setting up here – it's not easy."

With that still calm yet serious expression on his face he began to talk about the way he had started and the things that had happened up to the time when he realised that his idea had crossed borders that he never could have imagined possible. The journey had never been plain sailing. What can now be seen as a leading business has overcome a long succession of hurdles and effort: thousands of hours of tireless work, unyielding demands, pushing on to breaking point, etc.

While Amancio was reliving unforgettable moments in the life of the company, it occurred to me that I might ask him to tell me something about the incidents in his international career that had been most memorable. There was no hesitation. He began his tale, neglecting not a single detail. "The day I arrived in Paris, in 1990, shortly after opening the first shop very near the Place de l'Opéra, I ran slap bang into a spectacle worthy of the building that stood behind me. In the capital of fashion, in that world bursting with luxury icons including names like Dior or Chanel and are uttered with the most profound reverence, a pathway was being forged with surprising energy by a new way of looking at fashion, a perception I always felt was possible, yet somehow incompatible with that environment in the cradle of glamour. What I had to do was strive to my utmost to spread a business model that was already a reality in Spain and Portugal, based on the best possible quality/price ratio as far as possible. The innovation that was a revolution in the market was to arrange matters so that people of all social levels could dress well. That was the great height to which I aspired, but I could never have imagined what lay before me. When I tried to walk into that first shop in the French capital, I couldn't make my way through the solid barrier of people queuing in the street. I stood there in a doorway sobbing like a kid. I couldn't hide it."

Amancio Ortega's European dream was taking very sound steps forward in remuneration for the hard work and iron discipline that had always been supplied by the man himself and everybody who believed in his project. The boy from a village lost on the border between Asturias and León was turning an impossible dream into reality: he was conquering Paris – or, at the very least getting himself known in such an exquisite environment, even if he might not actually be a *haute couture* genius.

The spectacle of people expressing the height of elegance as they exited through that door in the Boulevard des Capucines with that satisfied expression of having found what they were looking for to base their wardrobe on or to satisfy their whim of the moment was soon to be repeated in the best streets of the French capital. This was a rare event that was soon to become a reason for pride, not just for Ortega, but for a lot of Spaniards who have yet to become tired of seeing Zara's unassuming bag, lacking all marks of sophistication, yet with the plaudit of worldwide recognition being carried through the Champs Elysées, Avenue Montaigne or the Latin Quarter of Paris.

New York, 1989

That situation was not new for Amancio, although the place and the experience were unique. Shortly before, in 1989, he launched himself on the other side of the Atlantic. In the city of skyscrapers, the melting pot of civilisations and trends that the heart of New York has long been known to be, and that still is, he experienced something rather similar to what was to happen a year later in Paris.

When he told the story, it was a very peaceful afternoon in Arteixo. To tell the truth, you seldom have any impression of haste or frenzy at the Inditex head office. That's why talking with Amancio is always unforgettable and a way of coming into contact with the greater world which is usually driven from the company's headquarters. You learn a great deal from the peaceful sensation that always accompanies the memories reverberating in his brain like the magic of an unfinished symphony; tales he never ceases to recount while never glancing at his watch. "Who could have told me that my idea of distributing the product very quickly would stimulate such a response on the other side of the ocean where companies with the muscle of the GAP or Banana Republic are found? Among other reasons, I was unhappy about having to travel to the US because I don't like travelling by air. In Europe I made the majority of my trips at the time by car or train, but on that occasion, there was no other way but to fly. I can remember it as if it was yesterday – the moment I reached the corner of one of the biggest shopping streets in Manhattan where we had our first shop on American soil. I've already told you that my feelings tend to give me away. When I found myself facing the Lexington store, just a few steps from Bloomingdales, and I saw from outside that the place was bursting with customers, I could hardly believe my eyes. There were women of all ages coming and going, just like in a Spanish shop, trying on what they liked, looking, taking another look, feeling the clothes, disappearing into changing rooms and once they'd decided to buy, they patiently waited in an endless queue to pay. The assistants hardly had time to fold the clothes to give everything that feeling of order and attention to the customer that we try to achieve in our shops.

"It was yet one more occasion when I was overcome by emotion and I had to lock myself in the bathroom so that no one could see the tears streaming down my face. Can you imagine how I thought of my parents then? How proud they would have been of their son who had, so to speak, discovered America, starting from a little town lost in the sticks of northern Spain! Afterwards we opened more shops in the States, one of the last on world-famous Fifth Avenue, right next door to Gucci, a stone's throw from Saint Patrick's Cathedral and very near to the Sack's Fifth Avenue store. I can never really get used to it, although it doesn't produce the same impact on me that it did that first time."

From his observatory in Arteixo, Amancio keeps abreast of everything that happens in the Inditex store. As he puts it, "despite the resounding success that we had in New York, the US isn't really our first market objective, important though it is. In the big American cities, as you would imagine, both the businesswomen who fill the offices of the multinationals and the crowds of tourists who shop in the Big Apple are very interested in fashion. In the other states, women's lives are very different and they aren't so bothered." Ortega and his team could see it very clearly: while never intending to neglect this huge country, and with shops opening in Washington, Boston, Chicago and San Francisco, they were concentrating their expansion energies on emerging countries, particularly in eastern Europe and Asia.

Looking at Asia

In actual fact, international expansion is currently focusing on Asia. Amancio didn't actually attend the opening of the latest shops, "but I follow it very closely. When one of the managers arrives from our store in Shanghai, I never fail to ask with genuine interest, what is selling, why she thinks that her clothes are successful, and how she sees our business in China, Korea, Vietnam or Singapore."

This is something I've noticed so I told it to Amancio in one of our conversations. In Shanghai in April 2008 I met a considerable number of his 'Asia team', all young people with that special style that is very much the mark of the company. They would talk enthusiastically about their hard but fascinating work in that part of the world. I met them at a cocktail party that we had been invited to by Ágatha Ruiz de la Prada after one of the Luxury Brands Forum sessions organised by the China Europe International Business School. We were on the 85th floor of the Hyatt Hotel with an entrancing view of the most modern skyscrapers in the world lit up as the backdrop.

The Inditex people made a deep impression on me, because from that distant part of the world, however important the day's events might be, they still keep their attention focused on Arteixo in order to keep the Zara culture in a state of its purest essence so that it remains a reality, not a myth. One of the managers, María, at only 32 years of age, is the human resources head, responsible for three thousand staff members located throughout the Asian continent, and she travels from one country to another, opening new markets. Like so many others, she has grown up in the company and has taken her company responsibilities very seriously; in fact, she almost feels that the company is hers. She believes in the idea inculcated by Ortega that "no matter where you are, what matters are the people."

The same can be said of Víctor, another very young manager who lives in Hong Kong and works with this Asian conglomerate. He is aware of the importance of his position, opening new pathways through that world that is right now in the eye of the hurricane of big business. He does it without deviating from the fundamental course even by a single degree. He knows that the man without an office steers this company with the same certainty with which the captain of a ship moves the wheel. Although he knows firsthand what is happening far and wide within his empire, he likes to hear about it from the people who work in the various countries, because, as he puts it, "it isn't me making this company. It's the result of all the work of the many, many people who keep it moving forward from any workstation."

There is a lot of sense in this, but there is also truth in what someone close to him said after hearing his confirmation: "Of course we all built this company, but not one of our 80,000 workers would have been able to make Inditex without Ortega leading us."

Who is it who today decides on and leads the expansion into various countries? The people involved in day-to-day management assure me that while the president may be watching the business with slightly more physical distance, he still keeps a very close eye on it. In other words, he no longer explores a country inch by inch when he goes to open a shop there, as he did before. "When we come back from various cities where we operate, we discuss everything we've seen with him and what we're planning to do. It's one way of keeping him up to speed, and it happens in the most natural way possible, with no hint of the framework of an official 'debriefing', although we try not to neglect a single detail. This style of taking on board the guidelines of the company is the reason why the top managers of each department are fully involved with management decisions and can communicate them to whoever will implement them. It's strange that there is no 'royal we' here; it's simply that we've adopted a formula of describing what's happening without seeing it all in the first person. But it reveals a company philosophy, one that's firmly rooted here, whereby everybody takes responsibility for the decisions they adopt," is the explanation I receive from Jesús Echevarría, Inditex Communications Manager, a man who keeps a very close eye on international expansion. He continues by saying, "Europe was too small for us, although in the end we did manage to land in Italy. That was difficult for us for a number of reasons, although in recent years, growth there has been spectacular. And now we've jumped to eastern Europe and Russia, parts of the world where 'women like clothes more than anything else', as I've heard Ortega himself say. It's a question of mentality. Slavic women like to show off."

As I talk with Amancio about the continually expanding market, he reiterates the fact that Russia is a country that, apart from the fact that he knows it personally, encapsulates important perceptions of the future. In his opinion, the difference between the emerging countries in what is known as the BRIC zone (Brazil, Russia, India and China) is that in China, so far it is only Hong Kong, Shanghai and Beijing where there is any purchasing power. One hundred and fifty million people live on the eastern coast of China, and every year 10 million more achieve middle-class status and lifestyles, which is evidence of a remarkable rate of growth. "We also opened in Korea this year, and we are already well established in Thailand and Singapore. In India we shall be a little bit slower for legal reasons." I'm impressed by the way Ortega keeps up with the fluctuations of a market that is so globalised, so changeable and so complex at the same time. "What's happening in Russia is marvellous, absolutely amazing. We're no longer talking about a handful of millionaires, but a 20 million strong middle class all keen to spend their money and improve their standards of living. The economy is strong because of their raw materials. Next year, 2009, we shall open 60 shops there covering all formats. Whether it's because of the culture they have inherited or their love of beauty, I don't know, but the women are in love with fashion. There's a lot of artistic talent there. We shouldn't forget that Saint Petersburg used to be one of the great courts of Europe with a culture that communism was unable to eradicate." Shortly afterwards, Pablo Isla reiterates the fact that they would have liked to celebrate shop number 4,000 with the opening of a Zara in Saint Petersburg, but the premises were not ready, so Tokyo got the accolade.

International expansion in recent years continues to amaze Amancio himself. "I could never have imagined such an explosion when we started. But you keep travelling forward day by day and you see how at every step the road opens up before you." It should not be forgotten that Ortega was already 40 when he started as a businessman in 1975. Of course, it's true as we have already seen, that he had the experience of every step in the value chain: he was a manufacturer, a buyer, a store wholesaler, and he clearly understood – this is his brilliance – that the business consisted of incorporating manufacturing and the shop with logistics and design – two worlds which are theoretically difficult to combine.

Another key factor in the Inditex success story is the sure and certain knowledge on Ortega's part that you sell much more if the price is low. Customers are really delighted if they can find silk and cashmere items for 30 euros that cost 100 euros elsewhere. The shop with the latest trends beautifully displayed and at an affordable price, of good quality and with exquisite customer service is, it must be said, a Spanish success.

Last but by no means least, a basic factor is stock turnover twice a week. If to all this you add limited supply, the excellent location of the shops and extremely careful merchandising that takes place, you're looking at the reasons for Inditex's success.

Yet the question many people ask is how the same effect can be achieved in Barcelona's Paseo de Gracia and in an avenue in Hong Kong. The teams that launch the shops are the support and the launch is managed as their central focus. Nowadays a team of architects who have worked in over 60 countries prepare the projects on the basis of plans that factor in zoning and the image of the shops (to ensure that they all have the same feel), although not all are alike as the end result depends on the actual premises. Everything is decided in Arteixo and Ortega always takes a look at and reviews the work, a job he greatly enjoys. He passes it on, but as a team member told me, "we all ask for his opinion to see what he thinks about what we're doing, because it is simply a fact that nobody knows more than him. If you have the world's top retailer working for you," says one staff member, "ask him what he thinks."

Floating the company: before and after

During another of my meetings with Amancio in 1999, preparations were afoot for the public float of the company. The very understandable tension of such an important time for the company was palpable. I recall one lunch that José María Castellano was unable to attend, though he was fully involved with that crucial process. It came into my head to ask Amancio if he would be taking the company on the road when the time came, and he came out with one of the most cutting remarks I have ever heard from him, and it came from his heart with the tone of someone quite capable of fulfilling the threat, "If I am required to change my way of life, that's the end of the stock market float and I go back to my quiet life. Anybody who wants to know will already have heard what I've said: leave me alone to work, because that's what I know how to do. As for the rest, you can do as you please."

Amancio is a quiet man with enormous inner strength. I have always felt that he is very clear about what he wants at any given moment. When you ask him a question, the answer is always exact, and if he doesn't want to get involved, he is perfectly skilled in sidestepping the matter. I realised that on the question of the public float he wanted no more talk about it, so I shifted the conversation to areas where we shared interest. He gave every impression of being involved in something that he was completely opposed to, but that he was prepared to accept. He would listen, and add the last word.

At the time I was aware of the fact that he had to clarify and convince – no easy task – the other shareholders, family members and the 1,500 workers at the plant, department by department. He had to communicate to everybody that this step meant greater transparency, and that nothing would change; it was a business matter, nothing to worry about.

To find out more about the genesis of that decision, after the float I interviewed Marcos López, manager of *Mercado de Capitales* which was taken over by Inditex in 1999, specifically because of that decisive act. It was Ortega himself who explained the project to him. At that time the company was only present in a few countries. It had just been launched in Japan.

The procedure is engraved in Marcos' memory, minute by minute, up to the point where he tells me the facts in the present tense, as though they are happening right there and then, "From now on we are launching quite an interesting project regarding the preparation of the company, very much in line with what you know. As far as floating the company on the stock exchange is concerned, Ortega is not saying yes or no. He's letting things happen the way he does, but he still has the last word. I'm talking with him and with a number of the other key officers from the company to try to understand the picture. There are some for and some against, because they think a public float will cause the company to lose its character. It's a typical situation that happens in some crises, where some people get on board, and others don't. The root of the problem was that some very important members of the management team were not in agreement; these were people who are no longer with Inditex.

"There are three steps in the process of floating a company. The first is preparation, where I'm involved. Ortega has to let things happen. At no stage does he get a negative picture of the procedure, in fact quite the reverse. He is supported by people giving him good advice and explaining that this solution is the only way forward for a big company. But there are other people, as I've said, who don't see things like that, so to a certain extent I'm gambling. But at times like that I say to myself 'it's such a beautiful plan, it has to happen'. Ortega did insist on some ideas that were absolutely his own as the founder and president. 'This company is a commercial success and I want to make it very clear that the float should be such that the values of the company are reinforced. I didn't build it up and devote my life to it for a good many years for it to turn into a fiasco and ruin the image. Point number two: the float has to be undertaken in our style; this is the float of Inditex, not of the banks doing the organisation or of any other organisation; it's the Inditex float. It will create a very important appearance, but it is crucial that the business continue to do the same as it is doing now. In other words, floating the company is all very well and we shall have to keep an eye on the market, but it must not become the main focus. We shall listen to the market, of course, but we need not necessarily do what it says. We can't afford to make mistakes, putting financial values above commercial ones'."

Why did the analysts come here to Inditex? "We had four big global coordinators: Santander, BBVA, Morgan Stanley and Citigroup. Other businesspeople, some of them very important, convinced Ortega that he had to get used to the idea of being in the market: 'The stock will rise, it will fall, you mustn't concentrate on it, you just watch it from a relative point of view. You stay with the business side, as you always have'. The next point was to completely disconnect the commercial aspect of the chains, including Zara, from the float. Inditex was the company that was being publicly floated and the commercial network was not going to be used to sell shares. For Ortega, the shop is sacred; it is the temple of trade, of business."

Every initial public offering requires transparency. Discretion is obviously healthy, but not obsessive secrecy, and that was why it was decided to include the first photograph of Amancio Ortega in the 2000 report. The photograph was taken in haste, because he was in disagreement with the idea, although he understood that it was unavoidable. A local photographer was hired but failed to capture his personality. Amancio was caught with a very serious, austere look, as though he actually didn't want to have his photograph taken. The *Mercado de Capitales* manager continues: "In our efforts to get the company to be familiar with the market, we adopted a different approach to floating the company from the way we had done it before. A year before we asked five large banks to bring their national investors to Arteixo. A programme of visits was organised, they met the people and they were given a thorough explanation of what the company was. They were taken to Tordera, the Catalan logistics centre, and so on. With other companies it's set up like a blind date: they give you the numbers and it is as though you have to marry a stranger. This was completely different. The operations were explained to the large institutional investors, in other words, what is now known as 'viral marketing', and this followed from the initial movement. The investors whom we took such care with at the time later increased their participation making a clear commitment to the company.

"As you can see, the procedure was prepared with a great deal of care. In December 2000 we explained to Ortega what we were going to do, in detail, and gave him the 2001 timetable with three dates to choose from for the exact day of the IPO. The subject was discussed at the board meeting, and when it drew to a close, Ortega said, 'I like May best, so let's put it down for May. People are in a better mood'. It was a stroke of luck and intuition on his part, because the date was during the only month in 2001 when the market rose. Inditex was floated on May 23."

When he was asked how he felt about floating his company on the stock exchange, he replied, "It's as if my daughter were getting married tomorrow."

Typically for Amancio, he let events take their course and failed to be present in Madrid on the big day. But very soon he found himself impressed by the success of the operation, since this was the biggest retail IPO in the history of the stock exchange. As Marcos López puts it, "it was the most over-subscribed Spanish operation ever; in other words, demand over supply was the greatest in numbers of shares as has ever taken place in any Spanish company. With the greater number of foreign institutional investors, the operation was carried out without any kind of effect on the day-to-day operations of the company, since we knew exactly where we were going. The workers were given 50 shares per year worked, regardless of their position. A pattern-designer for example, who had been with the company for 20 years received 20 times 50, and a manager who arrived yesterday received 50. It was a generous and unique act. The greatest evidence of generosity on the part of a successful company is when the owner sells a portion of their shares to have them divided out among the workers. And that is what Ortega did.

"On 23 May 2000, the day of their share market debut, Inditex broke records and made a number of shareholders rich, including Rosalía Mera Goyenechea, whose 7 per cent of the shareholding was worth a fortune. Amancio retained 60 per cent, and the remaining 7 per cent was shared out among the other members of the family."

For Amancio Ortega Gaona, considered by *Forbes Magazine* to be the richest and most powerful of the "aristocrats of fashion," a very special group including Ralph Lauren, Luciano Benetton, Leonardo del Vecchio and Giorgio Armani, among others, floating the company meant that "the greatest danger is believing it. That isn't the culture of the company."

The best advertising

As far as the president of Inditex is concerned, the best advertising comes from efficient service – a service able to provide a flexible supply meeting all requirements. The supply should be effective in terms of opportunity, and this generates customer loyalty and excellent word of mouth. The company does not advertise through the standard channels. There was an aura of mystery that surrounded the president for a long time, that in the early days generated curiosity, which gave rise to endless comments appearing in the most important Spanish media, and which, thanks to the internet, soon reverberated all around the world.

Always sensitive to what is happening in the market, Ortega opened the first shops of a new brand devoted to accessories, Uterqüe, in July 2008.

6

The Customer is King

"You have to put the money in the shops"

When Amancio firmly states the importance the shop has always had in the management of his business, he is implicitly explaining another basic commercial reality in this time of such profound social change: it is the consumer who determines the order in the market, and if you want to succeed you must get to know the consumer, notice the way she acts, spoil her and lavish attention on her. I remember one long conversation we had about this factor that was to a large extent crucial to the success of Inditex. Ortega understood before anybody else that from a professional and social standpoint, the changing conditions of women's lives, his main customer, as well as the lives of families, brought a new focus in women's attitudes to everything related to consumption and attention to her image. In this new situation, fashion ceased to be a form of tyranny governed by the terrible question, "What should I wear?" Although it was an important and significant necessity, neither endless time nor money could be spent since the time and the money were not there.

"You have to give women what they want."

In the exciting new century when everything was moving at the speed of sound, the people who shaped the outlines of ideas governing fashion felt that a new way of looking at life through a different lens was going to change the course of the way women dressed. Amancio sensed what the market was asking for and completely devoted himself to the task of creating a basic product with the best quality/price ratio.

Without undertaking excessive contortions, the founder of this company completely absorbed the philosophy that was in the air by adopting the same rhythm as the great names of international couture. Donna Karan, for example, at around that time wrote a "woman to woman" letter in *Women's Wear Daily* in which she said, "As far as I'm concerned, the future of fashion will come down to style itself, not the dictates of a designer. It's my job to offer women freedom and the basic tools so that each one can blend them in a specific way on the basis of simple, timeless items of good quality, flexible enough to be worn from morning 'til night. This is what I think of current fashion – it's an affirmation of individual style. This is an *avant-garde* concept that, like background music, impregnates Zara stores from New York's Fifth Avenue to the Paseo de Gracia in Barcelona."

Amancio perceived it all with amazing clarity on one of his many trips across the world without precisely knowing the causes of what he observed. He told me on one occasion that, "We connect with the customers because we're seeking a *style* for woman. That kind of customer – of any age, not just young – is the kind who can walk into any place in Europe, Asia or America, certain that she can find what she's looking for not so much out of necessity but often based on a whim."

Another American, economist Carl Steidtmann, wrote in the *Wall Street Journal* that the change that was then taking place in fashion was the end of an era. The reason? Women wanted comfortable, practical, attractive clothing at affordable prices; a message that was being communicated in every language and that was percolating in millions of men and women who, in every corner of the world, were becoming addicted to the Zara brand and the other brands in the group. In Zara's shops they found a perfect combination of classical and modern clothing with an excellent price/quality ratio and a modern image that was easy to combine with a personal touch.

In December 1997, the director of *Women's Wear Daily*, Patrick McCarthy, declared, "For years we defined fashion as 'designer'. The big shift started quite some time back, and it happened little by little; fashion is what the market presented in these huge commercial chains. Classic styles, young looks, easy to wear, attractive garments that encouraged the most modern people to be cheeky enough to buy their clothes from chains like the GAP, H&M or Zara. A whole generation started to think that the most chic clothing was casual, and that there was no point in paying astronomical sums to dress. And then after the terrible 1980s other concerns appeared that were dominated by ostentation."

Inditex is the company that best understood what people were asking for, which is why it has occupied such an outstanding position at world level. The figures for 2008 show that their results had already overtaken those of the GAP and H&M. The reasons, some of which we have already mentioned, were obvious: they supplied a good product, an affordable price, they were ahead of the trends, and they changed the stock twice a week, a turnover that meant we didn't end up dressed in uniforms. And as if that were not enough, it diversified into cosmetics and products for "dressing" the house (Zara Home), with the thinking being that caring for the home is another of the great trends that had to be attended to. In mid July 2008, the group launched another brand with huge success, Uterqüe, devoted to accessories of unbeatable quality, good design and affordable prices, and soon, to be projected internationally. Accessories are increasingly influential in women's looks, since their dress may be as basic as possible as long as distinguishing elements are added. Amancio is very proud and hopeful regarding this new line which opened its first shops in La Coruña, Madrid and Barcelona, and which remains true to the philosophy of the man at the wheel of the vessel, "You have to grow to survive."

The personality of a woman triumphs over the miming behaviour of the consumer. Many people are tired of kow-towing to the dictates of fashion, and season-based trends are witnessing a gradual dissolution. We are living in an age when how you are permitted to look has become infinite, thanks to the appearance and juxtaposition of the most extreme styles. This is the reason why long and short coexist, classic mixed with the eccentric, a street look offset with the most refined luxury items. It is also beyond a doubt what explains the phenomenon repeated over and over again on the "golden miles" of the great cities, where luxury stores with the latest models of the season on show in sophisticated display windows, alternate with Zara's fantastic shops.

There has been a revolution, too, in new materials; mixtures of vinyl and plastic with silks and gauzes, the most daring colours with the most neutral tones. The Inditex sales team travel to the farthest limits of the planet attending all the fairs to find raw materials and buy from the best international suppliers, many of whom are Asian, to compete in quality and innovation with the giants of the fashion world.

Every style now has its place. As I said before, there is no longer one single fashion, but rather an infinity of suggestions and propositions that each individual will capture with good humour, a certain degree of rebellion and a healthy indifference regarding what is presented to us. Trends must be taken into consideration, of course, but on one basic condition: we must be allowed to dress ourselves with our own stamp. "We are not imposing a single line on everybody, but rather a way of living," Ralph Lauren has repeated each year when he presents his perfectly balanced and harmonised collections. And Karl Lagerfeld, designer for Chanel and Fendi, once said to me at one of our meetings after a Chanel collection, having observed what had happened to his experiment to design a small and affordable collection for H&M, that he felt that "we are witnessing the end of the star creators and the birth of simple, easier clothing that chimes with a free and intelligent woman; a woman who no longer slavishly follows fashion. Now it's fashion that follows woman." He told me that he "designed for a woman who chooses what she likes and is incapable of wearing anything else." In Barcelona, shortly afterwards, he defended the thesis that "today's structure forces designers to work with a management team." We should not, then, be surprised to find that on more than one occasion, these firms with their luxury designers to the fore have held talks with Inditex management and, indeed with Amancio himself.

It stands to reason that those who design must seek an effective balance and cannot be satisfied with mere dramatic effect. They understand that women cannot allow themselves to be overwhelmed by the latest trends, and that they seek to find what they really like among the thousands of items on offer. These are women who play an active part in society, who are not obsessed by appearances; women who are interested in the suggestions of the experts, but are increasingly influenced by their own sensitivity. The international catwalks offer us a world of colour, extremes and contrasts; delightful collections that are a pleasure to watch, but very far from the clothing we wear in real life.

If there are infinite kinds of lifestyles, there are also infinite styles of dress. This is not a call for anarchy, but instead, encouragement to develop an imaginative approach to fashion that marries aesthetics with personality, where quality is not forgotten. The great secret of finding your own style arises from knowing how to find what best suits the way you are and think, and of course, your own circumstances.

The woman of the 21st century is enterprising, responsible and independent; she is revealing her professional skills in every field imaginable from leading a nation to leading a great bank. And she must dress to match the way she lives, in the knowledge that a well-dressed person always reflects a balanced and realistic personality, because in the field of fashion, as in every field, the best indication of maturity and personality is being true to your own ideas. For that, all you need is imagination and good taste.

Amancio's shops are never empty

I have frequently wondered why the Zara stores in any city in the world are never empty. With a view to finding an answer to this riddle, I made a few trips to a number of them both in and outside of Spain, and without telling anybody my purpose, I began to collect information.

The most striking phenomenon is that the packed shop syndrome takes place at any time of day and every day of the week. The queues at the cash desk are the best evidence that Zara is not a museum but instead, significantly consumer focused. I have notes from places as disparate as Mexico City or Guadalajara (in Mexico); a huge corner location in a Jerusalem shopping centre or in the Paris stores, the Champs Elysées and the Latin Quarter, New York, Nanjing in Shanghai, Bilbao, Brussels, Vienna, etc. the list goes on. In many of these shops I talked with the managers who were holding the line hour after hour, attending to women of all ages who were coming in, looking, turning the garments over, trying on dozens of items, changing their minds, and – at last – buying something. "It's an exhausting job," they confessed to me in various languages, but a job that they strive to perform to the utmost the way the boss showed them. "Here the customer is queen, and we have to keep her happy."

What role does Amancio Ortega play in this commercial exercise? Many assistants claim to have seen him come into the shops incognito, and if recognised, he is said to ask not to be acknowledged. He was not visiting to see how business was going, but to encourage his people.

In an article published in the *Wall Street Journal* about the ins and outs of Inditex's success, and more specifically, Zara's success, the importance of the point of sale was discussed, and Elena Pérez was mentioned. She was the woman who for many years headed one of the first shops in Madrid on Velázquez Street. In that none-too-large but iconic space because of being one of the first in the capital, it is easy to find a range of people seeking to discover "what's new today", as you might at the opening of an art gallery. Among the elegant women of Spain visiting the shop are Princess Elena, Beatriz de Orleans and Nati Abascal, enjoying themselves by mixing a pair of Dolce & Gabbana trousers with a jacket that had just arrived on a lorry from Arteixo. Elena Pérez is the one who tips you off about where you can find what "arrived last night, and you'll like it, because it's just your style".

I met her quite a few years ago. She is one of those people who seem so relaxed. All she was doing was greeting and farewelling the shoppers coming and going, because they were already her friends. In order to find out how things looked up close, rather than from a bird's eye view, I planned to chat with her on behalf of a number of top level colleagues, to find out her impression of what it's like to run a shop within the organisation and also, what the founder and president was like. At first she put me off, which surprised me somewhat, but after a few days she called to invite me over. She explained that she would never utter a word without checking "up there" – in other words, in Arteixo – that they would agree with what she was about to do. That's what I call loyalty!

I like to highlight loyalty, a value that speaks silently about Inditex employees. I found the same attitude in all the people I interviewed to learn more about Ortega. Until the man himself gave me the green light, all I got was the runaround, with maximum politeness and a minimum of information.

Finally Elena and I managed to sit down for a chat one morning in the back room of the shop, surrounded by freshly opened boxes. "My opinion about Ortega?" She really knows him well, since she started working at Zara 20 years ago. And she gives me fair warning straight away. "I am incapable of being impartial. I have tremendous admiration for him, and I am enormously fond of him as a boss of course, but mainly as a person." Two things I'm keen to find out are first, to what extent does Ortega communicate the importance of dealing with customers in a specific way, and second, what is the role played by those in Elena's position who hold the rank of general manager. I have heard her answer on a number of occasions, expressed differently, but always with the same content.

"When I go to La Coruña for a break, not for work, I always make a point of saying hello to him. And we always have so much to talk about – he talks with me about the things that I have on my mind as though I were his only employee, and questions come up about what happens in the shop. It always makes me smile because he still calls me 'kid' like he does nearly all of us older staff, the ones he knows best. Even the new ones that he can't put a name to, they still get the same treatment. He asks about us with the affection of a father. 'How are the girls?' or 'Who's the new girl?' Now there are so many of us, just think how many of us there must be in the more than 3,800 shops he's opened worldwide. When I started there were very few staff, and we went over to the centre twice a year to see the collections and he was always there with us. As you'd imagine, times have changed, but he's still just as interested in what's happening."

Apart from this, her story is the same as what I have heard from so many others. Ortega is a boss who has always worked shoulder to shoulder with staff in shops and warehouses; he never hesitates to roll up his sleeves and help load the lorries if he is needed and that he is the first to arrive and the last to go. "And apart from being a good worker," Elena clarifies, "he's a perfectionist. It could be right down to Ortega himself to choose the button that will be put on a jacket. And let me assure you that this isn't just a pretty story we've invented to make him look good. I've seen him do it many times over the years. You'll hear a pack of stories about the way he is and the way he acts, as if it were something out of the normal scheme of things, something he did just once, but it would be normal for him. You'll meet people, for example who don't believe he eats in the same cafeteria as the staff, or that he can still be found strolling around the corridors of central headquarters to lend a hand if it's needed. Look at this photograph of one of the logistics centres," she points to one on the wall, "and there he is in the background, listening. That's what suits him best – he hates managing while sitting in a chair."

Ortega likes to take risks. Again, in Elena's words, "it was a risk when he started the business, and he's still taking risks. Every minute has to be a challenge for him. If something turns out badly, it will be Ortega who can explain it clearly to the team, or whatever department it is, and then act with strength to get the team to make the effort. He never raises his voice, but he still acts with authority and gets his orders obeyed."

Everybody agrees that the Inditex president inspires enormous respect, that he has a powerful personality and that he can appear very easy-going, but underneath that is real substance. Another area where there is full agreement is that there is nothing artificial about the way he is and acts. Although the phrase has been worked to death, many of his managers have accepted the fact that he has "definite charisma" and that when times are tough, the image of their boss sweating blood has encouraged them to hold the line. "If he's prepared to do it, I can do it, too, so I'm carrying on doing my little bit to keep this company moving forward." His example is inspirational, encourages people to work and shows them how to take responsibility. The proviso they tend to add is also important. "I've always seen him as infinitely understanding, very human, but a real father figure. In a way we are all his children."

Bisila Bokoko, of the Spanish trade office in New York, said that she was told by the first CEO Inditex had in the USA, that Ortega was "a human being of such quality that I'd choose him to be my father." Staff members like Elena Pérez, who had the good fortune to begin at a time when Amancio personally knew every member, never tire of talking about the way he used to deal with everybody without any hint of affectation. As the years pass, she insists that she still trusts him the same as ever, "It's mutual, because he'll suddenly call me at the shop about something that worries him, not about the business but about me."

The example she gave me is very telling. For a number of years, Elena travelled around the world, helping to open stores in various cities. As the workload grew she found it increasingly tiring, and needed time to rest. She passed the message along the line to human resources, but it was Ortega himself who immediately called her to tell her that he was aware of the situation, perfectly understood what she needed and that "we shall have to organise the others so that you can get a bit more time to yourself." These were the lean years, when belts had to be tightened. The company was expanding fast and the shortage of people was pressing. Yet it was Amancio who personally handled the matter. "What exactly would you like, what do you need?" he asked. Elena explained that if she could get her Saturdays back, she would have the weekend to recover, and Amancio was in full agreement. "His genius is being able to blend a very demanding approach with putting himself in other people's shoes," is how she put it.

"Why is it that in some cities the 'staff wanted' notice is everywhere?" I asked her, aware that some people think the hours are too long, the pay too low and the customers frequently less than polite to the staff. "We do work hard, of course," Elena says, "but I think the company is very fair when it comes to pay. We get paid a base rate and on top of that we earn commission – the sales staff are paid a percentage on overall sales, and managers receive bonuses. Ortega has a sense of fairness, and I can assure you that it doesn't stop with wages but extends to every aspect of his life."

The most striking aspect of this man's generosity, and any number of people are willing to repeat this, was the way he gave away shares to all the employees when the company was floated on the stock exchange. For many people, that decision was crucial. The money, which soon grew, was devoted to a variety of purposes, from helping parents buy a car to opening a current bank account for their children. In the case of Elena Pérez, "I was just about to buy myself a house in the country, and that was the financial push I needed to be able to afford it. I told Ortega as much, and he said, 'Great, Elena, now you can really enjoy the extra free time you have over the weekends!' He hadn't forgotten what I'd asked for years before. What a memory! He forgets nothing."

I have to confess to a serious doubt as to whether a company growing at the rate of Inditex will be able to maintain a philosophy where the human side of things takes priority. Obviously, things will change, because there are now so many shops and the staff number in the many thousands. If you add in the cleaning staff, transport workers and all the other people who work for Inditex indirectly, the number is close to a million and a half.

I ask Elena if the Amancio she knew at the start and today's Amancio are the same, and before I have even finished framing the question, her answer is, "Just the same; a simple, friendly man. He has allowed none of it to go to his head. I met him when he was still under 50, in the prime of life, and now at 70-plus he's still attractive, with his smile, his look, the warmth he communicates and the impression he gives you that as far as he's concerned, we're part of his family. The company grows and grows, but he still gets about in the same style of shoes, shirt and trousers." And what she says a moment later makes me smile, "I know that he'd like to wear Zara more often, but sometimes he gets annoyed with the men's department because they don't have his size in trousers. As a person, he's just the same. I still see him up there in Arteixo every year. And now and again, down at the shop in Madrid."

When Ortega's wife, Flori, shows up at the shops, she's just another customer. Sometimes she comes just to say hello. She never comes to check on how things are going. Nowadays she's recognised because her photograph has appeared in the press, but until quite recently nobody paid her any attention. "A customer once asked one of the assistants what Amancio Ortega was doing here. She had to tell the customer that he was the owner. Yet you could never have imagined it, he was just strolling about like any other customer's husband." She continues, "What I'm trying to say is that Ortega is *unusually* normal. And the same goes for the entire family. One Saturday he suddenly appeared with his daughter, Marta, who bought and paid for a jacket she liked just like any other customer. Marta is just as straightforward as her parents. Everything she does, she wants it to be the best."

I seize this opportunity to ask the manager of the Velázquez Street store to tell me what she thinks her boss' attitude is to money. "It's not important to him. As far as he's concerned it's just a tool so that he can create jobs. He opens shops or launches new chains not so that he can make a fortune but for the satisfaction of creating jobs, and so that people can enjoy a decent standard of living. And in the meantime, his own simple life, his family, his friends, never change."

"Does he have much influence on what they manufacture?" I ask.

"Of course he does!" I have heard this point of view from as many people at the points of sale as in other areas of the company. Ortega has always carried weight when it comes to making decisions regarding the product itself as well as about the method whereby it is brought to the consumer. Today, his opinion still matters. He is a groundbreaker, making his way into the future.

Good quality clothing?

Some people still have the idea that "Zara clothes are cheap, but of poor quality," a criticism I pass on to one of the store managers with whom I talked when collecting material for this book. The response is, "The number of people who do actually think that is shrinking fast. There is even a section of the women's collection, for example, where very expensive Italian fabrics are used. These garments never make a profit but they earn valuable prestige for the company." At issue here are garments that are slightly more expensive, but still have a good quality/price ratio. At the other extreme is the Basic collection, produced using fabrics that are a blend of man-made fibres to keep costs down. Pure wool is obviously different from polyester or rayon, even though rayon can actually be a natural product.

In the opinion of the majority of the employees, Ortega had a very adventurous perception of the new woman and the paradigm change this implied. He understood that fashion had to become democratic, that good quality garments should be affordable by everyone, not just the financially favoured. "Our plan was to make clothes that were of steadily increasing quality at a good price and we succeeded."

Another question which comes up in my conversations with the store staff concerns the formula adopted to ensure that all the clothing does not come out the same. They are aware of the danger, and strive to avoid it in their shops. The starting point is at the production stage: they never produce a large quantity of units of the same garment; rather, they launch great numbers of models every year, around 20,000, with every effort made to avoid repetition. On top of this is the fact that all the shops are different. Some customers believe they are selling different collections, because the shops are run as though they were boutiques, particularly if they are small, so the feeling is that the clothing is exclusive. Store managers are allowed a great deal of leeway when it comes to placing orders to resonate with their customers' desires. The aim is to create a more personal ambience so that each customer is handled to perfection.

To ensure that everything functions with maximum efficiency, the shop manager has to be directly connected with the headquarters at Arteixo. All data is computerised and updated every night. At Arteixo the distribution staff works with the figures and the orders they receive for various shops. A significant factor in the success of the business is actually the relationship between the stores, so that they are able to interchange merchandise. Each manager is completely in control of what comes into her shop and what leaves it, and everybody else can receive this information in real time. The optimum is for a complete change of stock every 28 days. "The aim is that for every point of sale they put new stock on the shelves and transfer stock that doesn't move to other stores."

An ever-growing company

Many people were keen to explain that change has been unavoidable as Inditex has grown. Elena Pérez, who worked fronting a support team opening Zara businesses in Argentina, Brazil, Germany and Turkey among many other countries, says that all that travel was essential for the first shops because "at that time the company was just finding its feet and it needed a team of its own in each country. Support was certainly still needed for the opening of the second or third store, but now the support came from local staff. They are the people who best know their public, and anyway, you have to bear in mind what it costs to keep a team outside of Spain for any length of time.

"I remember that in Brazil," Elena continues, "the first Zara shop was being opened at a time when the country was passing through a very rough patch, economically. There would have been around 50 candidates on the preparation course, young women and men, and one of the young men stood up to say how grateful they were to Ortega and Inditex that at such a critical time, it was willing to trust them during the expansion phase. They asked us to communicate their gratitude which we did, but Ortega's never been one for flattery. I don't know whether it's because of his shyness or intelligence. More than once I've said something along the lines of 'What a beautiful collection, the customers will love it!' and he always cuts me off and says, 'OK, now tell me what's wrong with it'."

According to the Velázquez Street Zara manager, "growth also has its snags. We are now opening so many shops in so many parts of the world that it's impossible to travel to all of them. In the old days, when a new shop was being opened in Madrid, for example, all of us managers would go there to give a hand in the evening after we'd closed our own. Now that's completely out of the question. The business is an unstoppable snowball."

Human resources is naturally the section responsible for the selection of new staff. "When we need people we contact HR, which is very structured, and they send us the CVs of the people they have picked. We interview them and decide whether they are suitable or not. We managers have to work as CEOs; we are completely trusted in everything. If a shop doesn't work, naturally they will wonder why, but we are autonomous. Each department is provided with its own handbooks and training courses are provided for everyone, from the cashier on up."

Six fundamentals that govern the attention that should be paid to customers exist. They are known as 'the minimum six' and Ortega teaches them too:

- Always wear a pleasant expression.
- Smile at the cash desk.
- Have a pen in your hand.
- The manager is the person who should be attending the customers most.
- The changing rooms are an important point of sale.
- Everywhere in the shop: patience.

Elena continues, "There is a great deal of in-house promotion. Someone who has what it takes, if she keeps at it and works hard, will be promoted. If she needs to balance her private and professional lives, she can do it to perfection. We've been doing it forever, and not just with the most recent innovations; there were always half days, balanced timetables and so on, everything structured so that we could get more free time. There are a lot of positions to go for – manager, deputy manager, plant head, central cashier, coordinator, etc. In Madrid, 90 percent of the managers started as shop assistants. I think I was the last one to be taken on directly as a manager."

Zara Home

Some years after the boom that Elena was talking about, Zara Home was launched, the only brand in the chain to bear the iconic name. It was Eva Cárdenas, who joined Inditex to handle cosmetics, who initiated this new adventure in 2002 in perfect step with what was happening in the market. Home life and family life are of increasing importance in society. In Eva's words, "Fashion is a way of thinking, acting and living. It has a great deal to do with culture and the era we are living in." For some time now it has been noticed that people are investing more money in decorating their homes than in dressing. Donna Karan, Armani, Calvin Klein and all the great creators of international brands have taken it upon themselves to develop collections for the home, and some have even decorated hotels.

When Ortega decided to launch this line, the team responsible had everything ready to put before the board except the right name. The joke was that they would be the "nameless shops". They preferred Zara Home, as a natural extension of the brand, but the boss disagreed. He was well aware how serious the risk would be if things failed to turn out well. On the day that the pilot store was presented in Arteixo, Ortega was so moved that he called everyone who was at work at the time, from managers to warehouse boys, to come together and see it. Eva recounts that the question, "What will it be called?" could not be avoided. According to Eva, the team most deeply involved in the project were insistent that it had to be called Zara Home and that it would be a success. Ortega remained unconvinced. Despite their desperation, he replied that they had to make a living. Since the work of transforming the concept into a good product was so difficult, it could not be allowed to fail just because of the name.

"Finally," she continues, "after endless insisting and discussing, on the day that we were celebrating New Year's Eve in 2002 he came to see us, grinning from ear to ear, and said, 'What will you give me if I let you call it Zara Home?' 'One big kiss!' we all answered, thrilled by that display of trust. We assured him that we wouldn't let him down and so it was that on 1 August 2003 we opened the first shop in Marbella. There had been a setback that prevented us from following the tradition of opening in La Coruña, but it was still a complete success."

Eva is another of the great personalities who have been behind Amancio. She confesses that what she really finds wonderful is that "you end up thinking that it's your own business". Ortega manages to get people to follow him because he is a *real* leader, one who leads by example – a man who puts his shoulder to the wheel, knows how to delegate and gives you complete responsibility. "More than once," she says, "when I was unsure and I asked for his opinion, he said, 'And why are you here? You have to learn how to make those decisions'. In reality, he's behind everything and involved in everything, but he trusts you from the word 'go'. He's straightforward and friendly, nothing like the cool managers you often meet, and he blends a sense of humour with high standards and that's something you grasp from him. He's never satisfied and you absorb that desire to continually outdo yourself, to keep moving to more and better things."

Another factor which Eva Cárdenas highlights is "his amazing memory. He never forgets a thing if it's to do with people and the company. He possesses extraordinary special perception: he can look at a plan and know what the shop will be like when it's working. He runs rings around the architects." I ask her how she thinks Amancio developed these skills, and her reply is that he has a sixth sense when it comes to quality. "He can glance at a thousand garments hanging in a bay and immediately pick out the best ones. He's like that with food – he's passionate about excellence and beauty. That's why Inditex is what it is."

7

An Ethical Project Made to Measure

Amancio Ortega is looking tanned and healthy on the last day of August 2007. While half of Spain is on its way back from holidays, he receives me in his command post in Arteixo wearing the broad smile of someone at peace with and in his life. He steps up with his usual confidence and gives me a natural, pleasant greeting, just to say that he's glad I've dropped by to say hello. Things are at a very exciting stage. His image in the national and international media as the genius of the textiles and distribution industries of the 21st century and the brilliant head of a pioneering and revolutionary business in the world of fashion is constantly growing.

During those final days of August we witnessed the earthquake that devastated Peru. Almost immediately, the press was saying that Inditex had contributed a million euros to ease the tragedy to some degree and help the victims. I found out that subsequently many more companies added millions to this humanitarian aid action, impelled by Ortega's gesture. It was an obvious example of the enormous influence that Inditex, or in this case Amancio, its president, exercises with every move he makes, and not just in regard to his sector, but in everything he does or promotes.

That morning before returning to Madrid, I had the opportunity to congratulate him on the speed of his response. This was the opening move of a fresh exchange of impressions about life in general. I know that every time we sit down for a chat I have to reassure him yet again that he need have no fears about airing his opinions to me. "I'd like to be a witness to the influence you have, and of how responsible you are in all your actions," I said as we shook hands. I continued to remark about his ability to beat records, not just when it came to achieving business figures of astronomical proportions, but also in the business of responding so quickly in so many areas, such as contributing aid to the third world. I told him that as soon as I heard of his decision I called his Corporate Social Responsibility manager, Javier Chércoles, to ask him how the aid was being channelled. He replied from Lima that Amancio had not been satisfied with sending a healthy donation to the site of the tragedy and had ordered some of his people to go over there straightaway to collaborate on the spot to do what they could in the face of such massive destruction. They were working around the clock with a variety of NGOs, ensuring that the aid was getting to where it was needed most. This contribution of aid turned into a new experience. Ortega agreed, "Yes, someone had to clear a path. But I do things because I want to do them, not to be gossiped about. There's nothing I need. What I've done here, I've done; I don't have to go around in circles about it.

Ortega and a commitment to a community enterprise

Javier Chércoles joined us, fresh from his return from Lima. It gave me an opportunity to ask both of them about their perceptions of Corporate Social Responsibility (CRS), something fundamental to a company of the calibre of Inditex. Javier said that when he heard about the earthquake, he rang Ortega. Apart from the fact that Inditex has a manufacturing plant in Peru, it is also deeply involved in carrying out and subsequently working on initiatives that are known as the "Community Development Programmes," particularly in the field of education. After a brief and to-the-point telephone conversation that covered a predetermined action plan, he asked Amancio for the green light to donate funds to Peru's emergency programme.

Ortega's reaction was instantaneous. "He asked me who we were going to work with, why there and not in other settings with similar disasters, what sums would be involved and also whether I was planning to organise other types of actions. The first response set his mind at rest – the actors responsible would be those who could guarantee immediate aid to alleviate the suffering of the victims of the catastrophe in a way that was transparent, effective and secure; in other words, the operators would be his good friends and advisers from the *Fe y Alegría* (Faith and Joy) NGO who had never let him down, and who on this occasion, along with Caritas, deployed the "basic Christian communities" and their parishioners to manage the aid that would arrive over the following days. We sent support to Peru along the lines of what we did with the *Prestige*, in Sri Lanka and in Morocco, where we worked and developed some exemplary projects."

By way of support, someone suggested an idea that caused Ortega to hesitate for a moment: they would have to publish this particular action in mass circulation newspapers. Ortega is very unhappy about publicising what he does, and that is partly on the grounds of that very fundamental and highly respectable Christian standard he has always held to – "never let your left hand know what your right hand is doing." However, he accepted the proposal. If Inditex publicised this news item, it was highly likely that other Spanish multinationals would follow his example and take immediate action. He understood and his answer was immediate, "Agreed, but call Pablo Isla. Tell him about it and if *he* is in agreement, then go ahead."

There were barely four minutes of telephone conversation, one person in Galicia and the other in Valencia. By then Ortega had framed a complete strategic action model for a complex catastrophe, but perhaps the most important thing was his decision to send his top CSR executive out to manage the start of the programme in the middle of August. It was important, in real terms, to "be there". A fast and logical decision, the outcome of good common sense due to his clear perception of just what social responsibility involves.

We chatted for quite some time about social responsibility. Javier, who talks at the speed of sound and cannot be interrupted, is a great expert on the matter, and can explain it with all the detail you could ask for. He believes that his president is a man who gives absolute liberty to anyone he trusts. Chércoles explains that "Ortega is one of very few people who allowed me to develop as many ideas as I want in order to shape the model of a sustainable business. He has never put hurdles or obstacles in my way. When we were planning to implement the first sustainability report in 2002, he asked me to give a four-minute presentation to the management committee to justify the decision. Most people were against the idea, because we would be the first to be disclosing company secrets; our competitors weren't prepared to do that. It was unnecessary and uncalled-for according to one of the executives present. On the rather more complex question of the defences of the preparation of the report, Ortega intervened: 'You've understood nothing. It's the world that is calling for this. It is being asked of me, and therefore of Inditex. If we don't get on board now, we're going to miss the boat. Excellent presentation. Go ahead,' he concluded. The outcome was that this company was the first Ibex-quoted corporation to publish its report."

The corporate social responsibility department arose from a presentation made by Javier Chércoles for José María Castellano in March 2000. At the time he was working as a director of a strategic consultancy with PriceWaterhouseCoopers on behalf of other textile brands including the GAP, Timberland, Sara Lee and Nike. He was also collaborating with the London office to develop a British Petroleum project. His senior partner asked him to prepare a proposal for Zara, in La Coruña and Chércoles asked him for a free hand to do something innovative, since Inditex had never used consultancy services. To prepare the presentation, he made use of a dinosaur programme for children that he had bought the night before in Trafalgar Square and based his presentation on that.

Everything revolved around the "bites" that the dinosaurs, raptors were taking from the reputation of the corporation. Each raptor had a Latin name, and each stakeholder shareholder was associated with a similar name. *Raptors* and *stakeholders* were the participating parties. There was a short account basically saying that the "interested parties" could bite as they saw fit. In other words, when they "bit" they didn't negotiate – they were doing it just like the tyrannosaurs of the Jurassic period. This was pure provocation, but there was no possibility that Inditex would ever buy a strategic consultancy project otherwise.

Chércoles apologised if the content of the presentation seemed rather cheeky. He explained to Castellano that, if at any time he happened to offend him or the company he represented, he could make another more conventional presentation. But Castellano let him go on. The cry of the first raptor took the number two person at Inditex by surprise; it was the cry that would later allow the CRS project at Inditex to develop. Fortunately it turned out that it coincided with a particular corporate preoccupation at Inditex and in the final analysis, with Ortega's strategic decision to float the company.

The strategic consultancy project for the drafting and tailoring of a code of conduct was later passed by Ortega. It began in September 2000 under the title, "An ethical project made to measure." Among other activities, it included doing interviews with over 40 top Inditex executives with specific questions related to ethical aspects of the company business model. Everything proceeded according to plan until the day when Chércoles had to hold his interview with Ortega. Javier told me that he bought a Zara tie for the occasion, and when he let slip where he had acquired it, the boss commented, "it doesn't really suit you."

The meeting, planned to last a quarter of an hour, went on for more than three hours. Ortega started by trying to find out a little about Chércoles' private life – who he was, what he was doing, what he wanted out of life, etc. They talked about his family, his religious and ethical beliefs and his value system. It turned out to be a full x-ray of the man who some months later would be invited to manage the first corporate responsibility project in Spain.

Over that lengthy period of conversation we covered matters such as the upcoming public float of the company, the effect it would have on the life of the corporation and on his own life and future challenges to be faced. Before we called it to a halt, I asked him what the goal of his work was. To find an answer for such a direct question, Javier Chércoles fell back on a Brothers Grimm story, *"Fearless Youth."*

There was once a young man who was afraid of nothing but there came a day when a witch cut off his head and he saw himself. From then on, he knew the meaning of fear. Ortega laughed at the explanation. "If that's your plan and you can show it to me, go for it!" he said.

This was in November. This conversation had immediate consequences: a complete about-face had to be taken regarding the final objectives of the project and also the matter of ensuring that it was being observed in the short term. In other words, if it had passed by the board of directors at that time and the outcome of the check on compliance was published, there might have been problems. To achieve this, Chércoles focused all his efforts on visiting the factories of suppliers in Morocco, Portugal and Spain – an exercise rather different from his conventional consultancy work.

The first draft was delivered to the management in February 2001, and after revision by independent consultants the report was submitted. Ortega congratulated them on the project. When Chércoles went back to his office, he received a telephone call inviting him to take part in the Inditex CSR project. Three weeks later, he joined the Inditex team.

Very soon afterwards the first strategy for setting up an Inditex CSR model was presented. For this purpose, a presentation that included two options was used. One was very ambitious, involving deep-seated changes and dramatic short-term effects, while the second was conservative, would involve slow-moving changes and follow the examples set by other companies in the sector. In the wake of initial hesitations expressed by the board, Ortega was very clear – "Let's go for the difficult one." Once passed by Ortega himself and the Inditex Board of Directors, the plan underwent no significant changes. It was a strategy that included, among other things, the offer of a unilateral and unique commitment to change and a new way of developing a sustainable business model when the concept of sustainability was still largely absent from corporate strategies both inside and outside Spain.

The commitment became reality and membership in the United Nations Global Compact platform was signed; Inditex was the first Spanish corporation to adopt this commitment on a voluntary basis. "What a fine mess we've got ourselves into!" commented Ortega.

"All we have to do now is work, work and work. Nobody will let us off if we fail."

Another of the actions foreshadowed in the strategy was the proposal to set up a social council that would report directly to the Inditex Board of Directors, and hence to the corporate "good governance" organisation. At the time, this proposal coincided with the first purchase of shares in an Ibex 35 company by SETEM shareholders to exercise what is now known as *contestability*. Yet again, Javier Chércoles sought the support of Ortega. Within the company, voices were raised against the project, particularly about the speed with which things were happening. The NGOs, the shareholders, journalists – everybody was questioning the Inditex model.

The only tool available to correct this kind of situation was to increase transparency. Amancio understood this and it became clear that a consultative body would have to be set up by institutions in the third sector; organisations that up to 2001 had very little to do with the reality Inditex was living, as did practically all of the companies in the Ibex 35. It was still difficult to put it into practice six years later. The council is a reference model for regulating relations between the third sector and the harmonious establishment of the Code of Conduct of Inditex External Manufacturers and Workshops.

The worst moment was after the destruction of a textile factory in Bangladesh. The factory collapsed in Savar, central Bangladesh, as a result of mistakes made in the concrete mix. As it happened Inditex had only produced 30,000 items there at the time, but the number was irrelevant. Nor did it matter that it had been an Indian trader who, without having received permission to do so, had "moved" the production of 30,000 children's polo shirts for South America's southern cone summer campaign from India to Bangladesh. Other huge multinationals in the textiles distribution field were producing millions of units at the time of the disaster. All this was of no importance. The only thing that mattered was that Inditex had been manufacturing there.

Ortega's words to Chércoles were, "Do everything you must to fix the situation. I don't care about the press, what matters is resolving the crisis immediately and effectively. And help the people. If they need us, let's help them." Javier immediately set off for Brussels to meet Neil Kearney, General Secretary of the International Textile, Garments and Leather Workers Federation. He had a direct mandate: Inditex was ready to resolve the crisis whatever the cost and to set a precedent for any future actions. At hearing this, Kearney's expression changed. It was the first time he heard statements of this nature coming directly from the president of a textiles multinational. He accepted the challenge and withdrew from the offensive.

Chércoles and Kearney travelled to Dhaka. With the main local unions, they set up a task force whose job was to assess the damage and establish an initial action programme to alleviate the immediate suffering of victims and their families. Within two weeks all the injured were evacuated to private hospitals. Investigations were set in motion to work out whether it would be possible to design a pension fund to deal with similar situations in other locations that would be answerable to the CSR and checked by teams from organisations of acknowledged international prestige (KPMG International).

A number of the large international corporations in the retail and distribution field were against this. If the Spectrum Voluntary Relief Scheme fund were set up, it could be reused in the future and this would spotlight all the risks this could imply for the industry.

Today the Spectrum Voluntary Relief Scheme is a reality as an essential action tool for calculating damages and physical outcomes that result from accidents in the workplace in the third world. In real terms, it is a key element for managing and negotiating in similar humanitarian crises to what happened at the Spectrum factory in Bangladesh.

In the wake of Spectrum, other types of projects emerged, such as raising the minimum wage for the country. Perhaps the most important outcome was that moves were organised to establish and defend the rights of association and collective bargaining in the factories of the Inditex providers. As a result of these actions, over 2,800 trade unionists in the third world were allowed back into the factories of their suppliers in very complex and disparate geographical scenarios such as Peru, Morocco, Turkey, India, Bangladesh, Thailand and Cambodia.

This led to a new concept of the business model. It may well be that we are witnessing a paradigm change involving both action modes – equal representation for local and international union representatives, global level buyers and employer organisations – and methods of dispute resolution via the creation of a trade union capable of developing "mature industrial relations between all parties involved".

Equally significant was the signing of an international agreement between Inditex and the World Federation of Trade Unions to jointly oversee the appropriate incorporation of the Code of Conduct of External Manufacturers and Workshops into its production chain. The trade unions were invited to be involved in the processes of establishing and supervising the two main key points sought by the major agreements of the International Labour Office: the rights of association and collective bargaining. What this means is the existence of a unique and innovative agreement that until then, nobody had the nerve to sign.

Again, Ortega supported the project. He had to be there, to take that step forward and make a commitment. Following the signature of the agreement in 2007 by Pablo Isla, Ortega took part in subsequent private discussions. The guests were Neil Kearney and Fiteqa (Textile, Garments and Leather Workers Federation representatives).

I, myself, am a witness to the fact that Pablo Isla, in a lecture for former students at the ISEM Fashion Business School, explained the Inditex business model and produced a magnificent presentation on a range of very innovative store projects in Spain run by the physically and mentally handicapped. This is yet another example of the company accepting its commitment to social responsibility as a starting point for its business model rather than as a final or additional feature of its profit and loss statement.

The goals of the CSR are not economic. Social responsibility is present in all group procedures as a logical factor that is built into the company in general and in particular, as regards the communities where it operates. It is astonishing to see how production chain upgrade programmes have increased the productivity of the suppliers. This is no mere lip service paid to political correctness; it is a part of the DNA of the group and its entrepreneurial culture. Inditex has initiated a process of commitment to change at the most humane level. It is based on transmitting, encouraging and respecting human and labour rights and reaches down to the over 1,300 factories of its external suppliers. From a business point of view, it is via this process in collaboration with unions and their international federations that many entrepreneurs in developing countries have come to understand that change can be smoothly taken on board.

Chércoles enjoys explaining that the situation that was created using this formula is the outcome of a business model that evolves daily. It is the consequence of a very positive view that they can adopt, thanks to the ongoing dialogue with their interest groups in both industrialised and developing countries. It is possible to observe new relationships and roles coming into being between unions and multinationals. This paradigm makes room for sustainable social investment actions such as having stores run by distinct groups such as the mentally handicapped, the physically disabled and day-release prison inmates.

One aspect that those close to Amancio Ortega have found very satisfying is that this CSR strategy benefits not only direct employees of Inditex, but also the huge number of people involved in external supplier factories. It is an excellent opportunity for everybody for personal and business growth, because it offers them a new way of dealing with the future. Everybody, from Amancio Ortega and Pablo Isla to the last employee, is committed to the cause.

Success in a company with a heart

From time to time, Amancio hints that I should be less insistent regarding my keenness to broadcast our conversations. But I maintain that since I have had the good fortune to know what lies behind his company, I am under a certain obligation to report it. However, I would also like to set his mind at rest. With both resignation and trust in his voice, he repeats, "It's not up to me to teach you your job. But I would like it to be clear that if I have achieved something, it's because I believe in my formula and because there are a lot more people – thousands of them – who also believe in it. I can't know whether it would be the same for you. I often think that it would be great to completely change my appearance so that I could carry on being me with my same life as always, but with no one talking about me."

After this friendly introduction, now relaxed and on the solid ground of trust, we move on to other matters. I want him to explain something which arises from the very way he focuses his life – those enormously important factors that can never be pinned down by business schools nor taught in books. I tell him that his company has heart, and having made this claim I feel I'm asking him to talk to me about it. He seems disposed to go along with this, although at the start it looks as though he's going off at a tangent. "This summer I was talking to a big businessman who started when he was 13, just like me, and worked until he was 19. Then he studied for a degree and with a great deal of effort and sacrifice, he made something very impressive of himself. He told me that he sees good things in private life as well as in business as very simple. The most important thing is to keep it simple. And I think he hit the nail on the head. When you think about everything around you, carefully pick out the things that make you happy, you come to the conclusion that the most basic is the best. If you're lucky enough to realise this, it's as though you've won first prize in the lottery, because you're happy all day long. In this sense, being happy is easy. And what's good about this discovery is that you find you can communicate that happiness, that state of mind, that good mood, to your family, the workers in your factory and your friends.

"When you're at peace with yourself, you get home or arrive at the office in a positive state of mind and you transmit that optimism to everybody. Life is much easier than we make it out to be." After the briefest of pauses, he adds, "But you also have to ask yourself to come up with something creative, something different. Nothing is more satisfying than putting your heart and soul into something that you believe you *should* be doing."

This businessman friend of Amancio's (I didn't manage to get his name) left a very positive impression on Ortega. "We were dining here in La Coruña, delighted to be able to live in peace, free of fear and without bodyguards, because we don't go around making a show of what we've got. And we came to the conclusion that somehow some other people have lost the common sense you need to manage your life. Nowadays people know a great deal, in many cases have had a fantastic education, but there's too much ambition, and a terrible obsession to make money, money, money."

I shall never forget the tone of voice with which Amancio, the man who shows up on lists as being among the richest people in the world, commented on this obvious fact. Despite his position, he is able to look at the world around him with a critical approach that takes the form of profound perception. "Money has always existed, and in absolute terms it's an evil in itself. What has happened is that nowadays there is too much excess, and too much ostentation. This desire to own houses, cars, to take luxury holidays – it's all gone too far! People have lost their minds over it. They refuse to deny themselves a thing. Is it too late to get out of this fatal race?" But with a rather more optimistic and hopeful view he answers his own question. "I don't think it is. I'm hoping that people will realise what a mistake it is to let yourself be carried away by the consumer dream – no good can come of it. The main thing is to bring the children up so that they don't have that attitude."

Since we're feeling so comfortable with each other, I feel that I can raise the fact that his just-in-time clothing delivery formula is one of the major factors leading to clothing consumption, particularly among the young. Amancio lacks guile, so he accepts that, but he's also clever, and adds that my interpretation can be seen another way, "What we're about is trying to make fashion affordable by everybody. Of course, you're dead right when you say that it's the love of novelty that promotes consumption, but you have to accept that in our stores, clothing is not expensive and thanks to our formula, dressing well is an option for many more people, people who can do it without it costing them an arm and a leg."

This is the first time that I catch him admitting to his influence on the market in general. "As always, there has to be some banner to march under. One of the good things about our company is that lots of others follow us, they feel pushed in the same direction. Some don't just think it, they've actually told me – 'Either we follow your direction, or we disappear'. It's a fact that fashion has become socially democratic. Dressing well is now no longer a luxury reserved for the elite."

"Would you say that that is one of the main secrets of Zara's success?" I ask the president of Inditex. "One of the things that most helped us on the road to success in sales is that we receive information on a daily basis about what's happening in all the shops worldwide. The consumer is the one in command, and more so every day, and we've learned that you refuse to listen to her at your own peril." As we talk I find myself wondering, and at last ask if he ever thought that the future would be so glittery. He replies, "If we had had a clue about what the day-to-day work involved in this adventure was going to be, we wouldn't have had the strength to go on. I don't think I'd do it again. The sum total of the sheer weight of the work we've done over all these years is simply frightful."

"You have to love the people who work with us – it's an obligation!"

Ortega always speaks of his people as "the engine that wouldn't let him stop, not then, and not now. There are just so many people who owe their livelihoods to the fact that this thing worked! And they are all very much a part of me! I want you to know that I really love the people who have made the enterprise possible. I never stop telling my managers, 'You have to love the people who work with us, it's an obligation. You have to live close to them all, to their cares, to what they are, their homes, their families, not just their jobs. And then they give you their all. If you don't love them, you achieve nothing'. I always remember what my staff used to say to me when we closed a meeting. 'You take care of us, and we'll take care of the company'. If you need the people around you to put their shoulders to the wheel and you ask with affection and concern, you'll get everything you want, with interest."

When I ask how he ended up with these convictions and how he manages to communicate them, he says, "They're attitudes that you either have or you don't. It's a fact that you do have to go out of your way to acquire them. It's no good to proudly say, 'I did this'. You have to tell the truth. We all did it. What I'm really proud of is the fact that the people do their work and they really do see it as theirs. It's the same as when you have children and they're better at what you do than you are. The same thing happens with the people you train. There's no greater satisfaction than seeing that the people around you are making a beautiful job of what they're supposed to be doing.

"In life, if you devote yourself to doing what you believe in, and what you can do, you'll find success. But it's bad news if you find yourself with people who have no faith in what they have, or in the projects they undertake, or who don't rely on the kind of luck I had. Because working in what you like is a great piece of luck. That's the reason why I've always tried to find the most suitable situation for every individual, so that they can all enjoy their part of the work to the maximum."

As I've mentioned before in other chapters, Ortega likes to talk with his employees. "I like to know the people who're working alongside me. I've said it a thousand times, I don't have a big office just for me – in fact, I don't have a small one, either. I don't say that to attract attention or because it sounds good – it just happens to be the truth. I've always operated this way because I like moving around in the building, keeping myself abreast of what's going on. That's the way I notice that our quality is improving. In the women's division we now have an excellent recruit who used to work in Argentina and Mexico, and she saw right away what we were doing. I try not to lose sight of all those details, because it's the details that make the company. In this business people are cheering you one day and booing you the next, and you know it. The company works well because we're all completely clear about what we have to do. If we do that, everything carries on OK, or even better, day after day."

"Mr Ortega"

During one of my visits to Inditex, among the employees I talked with was a woman called Pilar Denllo, who spent a number of years heading up one of the factories, Sanlor which works for the head office. She told me in detail about the way the company had grown, but it might be better to say that she told me in detail about the way they had all grown together. She started when she was just a girl in one of the workshops, like so many other employees who have a similar story, and she told me of the endless days when Ortega was the one who put in the longest and toughest days to turn that embryonic workshop into the factory that she now manages. She cannot conceal her authentic admiration and respect for the boss. For her, more important than the bond of friendship that holds them together is "Mr Ortega".

"Can you see that the people really do love him?" she asks me, as though excusing her enthusiasm. "He really is everything you'd want in a boss. You won't find anyone say a bad word about him; not the newest recruit nor the woman who does the ironing. Nobody. People may have their own opinions about the company, but about him there is no disagreement, and you'll only hear good."

I tell her that Amancio himself actually said that if I was going to write a book, could I write one that wasn't pure hagiography, and so that's why I'd like to know what happened in the beginning. I mention the fact that I had heard rumours that he had paid badly and exploited the people in the workshops. Her answer is unhesitating, "It never happened. He is simply generosity itself. How dare they say that he exploited the people! I can assure you that he always said the same thing to the factory managers, 'Be nice to the workshops. Take care of the workshop staff. Always bear them in mind, because you', and he said this to me, 'you get the same salary whatever happens, but if the workshop has no work, they have no income.'"

Pilar emphasises that Ortega really insisted on the idea of responsibility, to the extent that she never stops thinking about social security factors and ensuring that her workshop is 100 per cent legal. "It's not so easy, because nowadays you can't find so many people happy to operate a sewing machine for a living like in the old days. I have workshops in Galicia," she continues, "and if the girls leave us, we have no way of replacing them." The fact is that the task is difficult in these hi-tech times, but at over 60 years of age, Pilar still insists that she's proud to work with a company such as this. "Sometimes I tell Ortega that it should be me paying him to work with this company. I remember one day when he thanked me in front of a group of people for working with the same level of dedication after so many years and still being excited by the job. He's a very emotional person at heart, and even though sometimes he has to be tough and take hard decisions, he has the humility to be grateful and the sensitivity to be interested in the last person he has met."

When I ask her to give me an objective assessment of the president of Inditex just before winding up our little chat, she says, "He's demanding, he pushes you, he makes you give your best. But working with him you can't help moving forward, because when he asks you for what seems the impossible, you find you can manage it even though you don't know where the strength will come from. He trusts you and knows that you'll deliver. And what happens is that you feel the company is you. Even today, now that we're not tripping over each other like we used to, the company has grown so much – sometimes a year goes by without meeting – we still get together every now and again at some meeting and I have just the same feeling that the company is me. We all feel that, and we've absorbed it from him. Working with Ortega, you grow as a person and as a professional."

8

How Amancio Sees his Company and his Life

A long lunch with the president of Inditex

I am welcomed in La Coruña in the first week of May 2008 by a cloudless blue sky. Once again, I have an appointment to lunch with Amancio Ortega, having now exchanged impressions with a number of his people over a period of a week. A stroll along the promenade is the best preparation for a chat with this man who seems as calm as the Cantabrian Sea, near Finisterre, where the ocean radiates strength and mystery.

This is a backdrop that reflects the personality of the protagonist of this book, someone everyone admires, yet someone who can have everyone trembling, not just when he's firm with someone, but – and this is much worse – when he ignores you. Like the wild waves that crash against the cliffs carrying everything without the slightest consideration for what drowns.

Our booking is for half past one, with the idea that we will have enough time for our conversation without rushing. Someone appears and tells me he will be a few minutes late as some urgent matter has come up. I'm told that he's very sorry about this unforeseen event, but he'll be right along. Indeed, in less than 10 minutes, in comes Amancio, as relaxed as always. The first thing he does is apologise for his lateness; as he says, he is very rarely late, and when he is, it is always a question of *force majeure.*

I remind him that at another of our meetings, he said, as included elsewhere in this book, that it was his father, a reliable railwayman, who inculcated in him the importance of absolute punctuality. "I like to be punctual myself," I tell him, "but there are times when something happens that just makes it impossible." Amancio agrees. "You're right," he nods, "but for me punctuality isn't just something I inherited from my father; it's because time to me is more valuable than it seems to be to other people. I think that making someone wait, regardless of who they are, is bad form, because it suggests that you place no value on time or for the person who is waiting for you. We have no right to make other people lose time on our account." His expression becomes very serious when he talks about someone he knows who gaily boasts about his absolute inability to arrive on time. "Some time ago, I actually had to put my foot down. I said, 'So and so, this is not going to happen again. Let me just remind you that I'm the president, OK?' That seemed to cure the problem."

This is the first time I've heard him say something of this kind. It almost seems to run counter to his usual approach of hardly ever talking about himself, as he would be very unlikely to pull rank. It would be as unlikely as him producing his business card (which, of course, he has never had).

We move on into the dining room and when we're seated he starts to tell me about something he has on his mind. I'm well aware that he rejects the idea that I might fail to communicate something crucial through an excess of personal admiration for him, but his tone of voice is still very serious when he repeats as though he'd never said it before, what I've already heard a thousand times, "You really must try to make sure that your story doesn't just focus on me. I can't talk to you about myself, or how I came to find myself in this situation. I would feel foolish talking about myself. For the umpteenth time, I have to repeat that Inditex is the story of many people. Once you've got that clear, talk to others who you think would give you a better picture. You'll find that if you have 10 people in front of you, each one will give you a different opinion, because everyone sees things from their own point of view." Fine. Perfect. I agree with everything he says and in return, I explain my own attitude, including the very lively interest being expressed by everyone these days about who Amancio Ortega is and what he's like.

He's a solidly-built man, carrying a few more pounds now than when I first met him, his hairline's on the retreat, he always wears a perfect shirt – white today, sometimes blue – and a grey sports jacket. He listens closely with the same understanding air as always. But on this occasion he seems to be on the defensive, maybe a touch more serious than usual; I might almost say worried. We fence about the balance between the trust that our friendship deserves and his keenness to protect his privacy. He finds none of my arguments totally convincing, because he feels that to a certain extent he is betraying his own principles. I wonder whether he will be able to maintain this position without losing his balance.

Vice-President and CEO Pablo Isla sits down at the table on my right facing the president. He listens to our conversation like someone watching a game of tennis when the ball is rapidly flying back and forth, a sport that both the president and I are great fans of. He probably wonders who will win the set.

"I understand perfectly what you're saying, Amancio," I say, maintaining the same tone of voice, "but you are simply going to have to accept what I've told you over and over again. Now nobody will be satisfied with a picture that appeared in a company report when the company was floated on the stock exchange, or the photographs of you with your daughter Marta at Casas Novas when there's some riding competition she's taking part in. People actually have a right to know who the man is who started this company that is everywhere now – at every fashion venue, every retail event and wherever the future of the textiles industry is under discussion."

I immediately suspect that I overstated my arguments, that I have swamped his ability to accept the idea behind my book. My argument was like a small crack in that reinforced parapet that Ortega industriously built up around himself. In order to make his position very clear and with the expression of someone who feels it is urgent to explain something that is of the utmost importance, he retorts, "There's something that really matters here that you don't seem to understand, and it's that I really am nobody special in this story." He continues with complete conviction, "I see myself as a worker who has had the tremendous good luck of being able to do what he wants in his life, and to be able to keep on doing it. That's the big story and the only story that I will allow to be told: what the work means. Along with this, which is my fundamental statement, one further matter arises, also of great importance: if there's anything I am proud of, it's the people who have come with me."

Now that we have the rules of the game cut and dried, Amancio is again the easygoing soul I've always known. It's as though these ideas well up from the deepest part of his being, and once they are aired he is free of all concerns and can express himself with complete frankness. "My success is the success of everybody who works and has worked alongside me. No human being can be so intelligent, so powerful or so arrogant as to think they can build a company like this single-handedly. There have been many, many people," his voice becomes lyrical, "who devoted their lives to this company. Many people," and he seems to be seeing them passing, arriving from the four corners of the world, "many people have helped built this wonderful reality, from the beginning until now."

Pablo Isla, then just 44 years of age, accepted the responsibility of his duties with complete dedication and enthusiasm just like so many others, such as Castellano, for example, as Ortega would say, who, for a variety of reasons, are no longer with him. "Finding professionals of this calibre," he bestows a grateful glance on the relatively new CEO, "is a gift from God as much as anything. Picking people is always a gamble. When you manage to keep the company on course, thanks to them, it gives you huge peace of mind about the future. This is real luck, and it has never let me down."

So when the time comes to choose managers who will be crucial for the company, what has he looked for since he took his first steps as president of Inditex? What does he feel he must know about them before entrusting them with key roles? His reply is emphatic, "What matters to me above all is the quality of the person who is coming to work for the company. I try to find out what their values are; I'm interested in their family life, their personal and human integrity that will be expressed in their professional capacity for the job they're going to do. But their personality is paramount. And I'm seldom wrong." How does he judge them? What does he ask of them? There is no scintilla of hesitation in his words. After all, he has spent many years surrounding himself with the best, and he knows very well what he wants. "A number of things, the first, the one that gives rise to others, is a serious sense of commitment to what they're going to be doing. Do they really believe what they're saying when they talk about how keen they are to come and work with us? I've always looked for people who will fit into the company, who will understand our values. One of our values is that responsibility demands quick action in any job. A problem must be solved without procrastination; you must thoroughly understand what I mean when I say that we consist of a network of shops with a company attached: everything we do is to ensure that the shop is focused on selling. We all serve the shop."

Despite his age and his position as an international businessman, Ortega is far from standoffish. He approaches you like a friend, and to a certain extent, he asks you to deal with him with that same level of trust. He grasps the truth of the people around him, and it is very important to him that they all have their own opinions. He expects people to clearly say what they think, whether or not he is going to like what he hears. He owns up to mistakes because he is flexible, but he operates with speed and not everybody can keep up with him. You realise why some people have been left by the wayside.

I tell him that I would like to know what he feels when he contemplates what his business means today. "Do you feel you made something of enormous scope? Are you sensitive to the fact that, thanks to you, fashion is now seen in a different way everywhere in the world?" This is a man who thinks on his feet, an expert in putting the ball in your court, "Hey, you, me, everyone who's a believer, and everyone who isn't, we all owe it all to God. Of course, in my case, I feel I owe it to God and to Inditex. This company still has a long way to go; there are no limits on how far. Certainly we're facing an economic crisis, but we should concentrate on the emerging countries: China, Russia, Brazil, the old eastern bloc, etc. From that point of view, the economy is getting better and better, because there are new markets with new consumers coming on stream, and we're holding all the production tools, logistics and distribution systems to meet their demand.

"If a company doesn't grow, it dies. A company has to be alive. I was 72 on March 28 and I feel that we can't stop growing. Nobody could ever destroy this company because the people we have working here are excellent and they are completely committed, from the staff who take care of transportation to make sure that the merchandise arrives anywhere in the world on time, to the people who create the designs for the entire production and those who are launching new projects. The company has to keep on being what it has to be."

What does Zara mean to Ortega?

"What does Zara mean to you?" I ask, since we have agreed that there are no holds barred. His reply is in the same vein. "For me, it means serenity, not a show. It's a brand that was born in a company that wanted to see the women of the whole world well dressed, not showing off. The same style of woman is to be found in every Zara. It's true that you always have to select a style because it just wouldn't be possible to take into account the characteristics of the whole world. You don't produce different designs for 80 countries; you design a garment that suits 80 countries. It isn't so hard," says Amancio. And because I know that he's fond of anecdotes about things to do with his commercial philosophy, he listens attentively when I tell him about something that happened one August day when I noticed a pure wool jacket in the Velázquez Street Zara that I thought was just perfect. Since the heat was hellish (42 degrees Celsius), I thought that it was hardly the right time to buy it and decided to wait until September, before setting out for Mexico. But when I went back to the shop, despite the fact that Madrid still seemed like the Sahara desert, the jacket had sold out! No matter how hard I looked in the other shops in Spain, there wasn't a single one left, not even in the display windows, which is usually the last resort. So I had to resign myself to travelling without it. Imagine my surprise when, upon arriving in Mexico City, I went out for a stroll in the evening around the hotel to clear my head from 10 hours in the plane, and found myself on the best street in the capital, staring at a fantastic Zara display where the jacket was in the window, large as life, as we say! I dashed into the shop ...what a let-down! That jacket had already sold out everywhere in Mexico and the one in the window was for a customer who was coming to collect it on the day they turned over the stock.

Amancio laughed, and said that, knowing the company as I did, I should have already realised that a fundamental part of the strategy was to never repeat a product, precisely so that uniforms could be avoided. "If there's a Zara garment that you like, you're more or less forced to buy it there and then or you'll lose it. The lines are universal and our customers have the same tastes, as we see more and more. To be successful, we just have to get the product right."

Amancio feels that it is fundamental to stay true to the Zara essence. "Again and again I've told my wife Flori, who was concerned with design matters for many years, as you know, 'I don't want anything in our shops to smack of luxury, that doesn't chime with the essence of what we are. What we're about is the real woman, the real public, not dreams'."

He went on to say that not long ago he went to check out a lamp that was part of the window display in one of the pilot stores in the main Arteixo building. He felt that this sophisticated lamp seemed unsuited to the product, and he was going to have his people to take it out. He said it seemed ostentatious and not really in keeping with the essential Zara. He talked to the project leader, gave a full explanation for his reasons for trying to stay true to the usual profile of good taste but without stepping outside the boundaries – respecting the DNA. The project leader said that on top of the fact that he had not felt right about the choice, he regretted the fact that he had been working alone on such a fundamental job, without a colleague with whom he could have compared his ideas with to achieve some kind of a balance. He confessed to Amancio that he felt rather isolated in this field where so much depended on imagination and creativity, so important for communicating the true image of the brand. "He was absolutely right. All of us who are responsible for not betraying the principles often feel that loneliness; we need people beside us to whom we can turn. We need friends."

When I asked him what it is that keeps him on the job after so many years, he replies: "Learning and growing. I keep on watching what is happening in the world and I keep listening. Until quite recently the rich countries were the Arab countries and Japan. Now it is Russia and China. In those parts of the world there's a definite percentage of the population with a great deal of money, and they spend it all, because it's a matter of easy come, easy go."

A weekend in Rome

Amancio tells me that he has just spent a long weekend in Rome, at the Spanish Embassy at the Holy See. That building, the oldest diplomatic representation in the world, was set up by Ferdinand the Catholic in 1480. The well-known Palazzo di Spagna gave its name to the famous Piazza di Spagna, always crammed with tourists walking up and down the stone staircase that rises to the church next to the Trinitá dei Monti. This jewel of Baroque style is partly the work of the sculptor Borromini, who also designed the extension of the building. The imposing staircase rises to the main vestibule of the embassy, where you are taken by surprise by two magnificent busts by Bernini, the "Blessed Soul" and the "Damned Soul".

Located in the historical heart of Rome, through the centuries the palace has been the meeting point of an exciting world, in which artists of all stripes mingled with Romans who made their way here to enjoy one of the spaces that is still one of the best known in the Italian capital and always throbbing with life. This palace has witnessed the comings and goings of guests as diverse as Garcilaso de la Vega, Casanova and the court painter, Diego Velázquez.

Various ambassadors who have been representatives here have been a part of the political history of Spain since the time of the

Catholic Monarchs until today, busy in Rome with the defence of such religious interests.

Although no one has actually brought the matter up, Ortega is becoming personally involved in the restoration of the embassy. The ambassador invited him there to spend the long Feast of the Immaculate Conception weekend in 2007 so that he could witness a traditional ceremony in which the Pope approaches the statue of the Virgin situated at the front of the Palazzo di Spagna. There, following an ancient custom, the oldest fire-fighter in the city climbs a staircase and crowns the Virgin. The Holy Father then reads a speech to the crowd packed into this historic square. The ambassadors receive the Pope at the door and then attend the ceremony from the balcony of the main façade. Amancio, true to his determination to never be the star of any show, turned down the invitation on that occasion, but promised to come later, and indeed did so in early February 2008.

He came back very impressed by the grandeur of Rome and the beauty of its streets because he had enjoyed the great good fortune of being able to visit the Vatican with his dear friend the ambassador, Paco Vázquez, who had many times been mayor of La Coruña. "Can you guess what someone said to me the day after I got back? 'Could it be possible that I saw Ortega strolling through the streets of Rome with the mayor?'" and he lets out a great guffaw. "You have to laugh, first because someone actually recognised me in the street, and second because someone called the ambassador of Spain 'the mayor'!"

Amancio admires Vázquez. They are good friends and he speaks with great warmth of the pleasure it gave him to be shown the corners of the Italian capital by such a high-class host. "Just imagine! I've been to Rome dozens of times, but always on business! I love that city more each time I'm there, but I can't tell you how different it was this past weekend!" He gives free rein to his memories by saying, "One afternoon we were invited to the Palazzo Colonna. Another wonder. And the way the prince and princess danced attendance on us! They were so perfect, because they were just so normal and yet so gracious. The best moment for me was when I met the princess and she told me that she'd always wanted to meet me and invite me to the palace because she was a great admirer of my work. When you think of the fantastic fashion available in Rome, with all those top international luxury firms, and here's this member of the highest level of ancient Roman aristocracy delighted with Zara! That just knocks me out. I never get used to hearing it. I always think that it can't mean me. When I told my friend Paco, he said, 'But do you know who you are?' and I said: 'Of course I know. And that's exactly why it has to be no big deal'."

I ask him if it's true that he's funding the restoration with his own money. Silence. An eloquent silence as they say, but since he can't deny it, it's a clear example of the way he likes to operate. Again, he hates showing off, and cleverly turns the conversation back to his travel impressions. 'You have to love beauty; it's one of the essentials of life. They know that very well in Italy, and you breathe it in the air. For example, when I looked at the façade of the Palazzo di Spagna, I realised that it had been painted in four colour tones that were very similar but in different shades. That's what gives it its amazing quality. Vázquez outdid himself during the three days I was there. For a start, when I arrived, they hadn't taken down the big Spanish flag that had been put up and flown to receive the Pope. Then he took me to see all the archives of the Vatican library and that side of the museum. We had a good look at a very tiny bit of Rome, because in three days you've barely started to see what this city has to offer. I was deeply impressed by the Pantheon and all those monuments that echo the ruins of vanished civilisations. It's a city that carries you back to the past. But the thing that most moved me was the Pietá statue in the Vatican. I find it impossible to believe that a human being could have been capable of creating something so sublime, so divine. The love that the Italians have for their city, for its history, and for beauty in general is truly wonderful. I really have to go back."

As the conversation proceeds, he confesses something that says a great deal about him. "It's during those very special moments that I'm aware of all my shortcomings. When people talk about my career they never miss out the fact that I started work at 13, and it's true, I did. But what isn't said is that I never had the chance to study, it just wasn't possible, and nowadays it's something I miss. To start working at that age, I had to give up a lot. It's as simple as that. My university is my profession. I wanted to be a different kind of businessman, to change the world, socially, I mean. And what I can say, looking back, is that I did manage to achieve that, because the raw material that Galician people are made of is wonderful stuff. Every one of them made an unusual commitment to my business."

The journey to Rome was not a business trip but "when I got back to La Coruña, the first thing I did was tell the others how impressed people are by our shops over there. Not to make them big-headed, but so they would understand the responsibility they bear. The Rome shops were bursting at the seams. I'm not used to seeing so many incredibly elegant customers carrying bags full of our clothes."

From the village in León to the world

"Things aren't as difficult as we like to think," he says, thinking aloud about the current situation. "When we look too hard, everything seems complicated. All you have to do is work, but work with passion. That's what my parents taught me, and they were just ordinary working people, the kind of people who saw hard times back then in Spain. They lived in the Basque country before the Spanish Civil War; then my father was transferred to Busdongo, the village in León where I was born. After the war they went back to the Basque country. I lived in Tolosa until I was 12, and that was when we made the move to La Coruña because, once again, my father was posted here.

"I went back to that part of the country when we opened the first shop in Oviedo. It's a tiny little village, barely half a dozen houses. I found someone who remembered us, although of course he didn't recognise me. Then on another occasion when we were travelling through a village in León, on the Camino de Santiago de Compostela pilgrimage we were recognised, but all they said was, 'You can see they don't give themselves airs'. They said it because there was another 'pilgrim' who'd gone by a few days before, surrounded by paparazzi doing a story that later came out in *Hello* magazine. I could never carry on like that. It's very important to me to be just one of the crowd."

I ask him which his favourite city is, anywhere in the world. "They're so different," he says without hesitation. "Right now I'm full of Rome and I'm determined to go back. I found Mexico City very interesting because of its past, but what a contrast between wealth and poverty! We have so much to learn! And with an eye to the future, Dubai is an amazing place, built between the sea and the sand."

When I wonder whether they have very many shops in that part of the world, Amancio's reply indicates that he's absolutely up to date with what's happening. "There are many of them in all of the Arab countries, but because of cultural complexities, they're all franchises."

Despite the fact that I know he hates to talk about his wealth, I have to wonder what it means to him to have so much money. His response is clear, "To be able to spend what you think you ought to spend without making a fuss about it; to be able to help a lot of people and their families live with dignity."

When a person has achieved success such as his and established this kind of situation in life, is there anything that can hurt him? "I don't think anybody can do me any harm, now. The past is the past. It's as though you're wearing a suit of armour. And anyway, I don't bear any grudges against anybody." Because of the absolute conviction of his answer, I'm afraid my eyebrows must have risen. "Really? Surely that must be impossible!" He corrects himself, "Well, if you're sensitive, you can suffer about anything, but at another level; injustice, for example. What you see happening in the world can drive you crazy. But the only thing I really can't tolerate at all is the slightest hint of an attack on my family. When it comes to the children, I give no quarter."

Then his expression softens when he remembers his mother, Josefa. His feeling for her is as deep as ever, and his eyes moisten when he recalls that woman who died at 94. "Flori, my wife, was with her almost to the last. She visited her every single day. I remember I once took her to see Marbella in my plane and she looked at me with that expression of admiration that only a mother can produce and said, 'Is this really my little Choliño?' She always called me that, and today my nieces and nephews call me Uncle Cholo. My father, in contrast, was a more serious man, as straight as a ruler. He died at 90. But the member of the family who loves me as though I were the last person on earth is my sister Pepita."

What is it that keeps you on the job after so many years? Are you the same man who spotted a niche in the fashion market? Do you still look at life with the eyes of an explorer? He laughs at my questions, but shining in his eyes is the truth of the endless years when he was 'first to arrive, last to leave'. It almost sounds as though he is excusing himself now, when he says, "Nowadays I don't arrive until 11, whereas once upon a time I was always there at nine, but I can do that because I know that the people that I've passed the job onto are extremely responsible, and everything is safe in their hands. They're quite capable of keeping the furnaces well stoked."

When the meal is finished and the coffee lingers and we can talk about anything we like the conversation turns to the current situation with the looming economic crisis. Ortega is not bothered. "You can't let yourself be scared by a crisis like this, you can't let it get the best of you, because it's fear that paralyses you. I remember when I was a kid and I used to come home late at night, a couple of kilometres from the station, and sometimes I felt so scared I could hardly move. Fear cripples you. You always have to take risks."

A Galician country house called Anceis

I change the subject and talk about Fernando Caruncho, a friend of mine and a great landscape artist who has designed gardens all over the world. I had heard that they were friends and that he had been involved in remodelling the famous *pazo* of Anceis. This old and aristocratic country house, now owned by Amancio, is said to be one of the most striking in Galicia. "It's a very pretty house from the 16th century. I use it as my country house, and yes, you're right, I did ask Fernando Caruncho to design a garden for me. I told him that I wanted cows and a smallholding, but this gentleman is much more refined than that, and he was determined to make a French garden. The outcome was that the project went nowhere, but we became good friends. I like talking with him when I can; he shows me things from the art world that he knows I'm very interested in."

One of life's little coincidences arranged matters so that a few days after my lunch with Ortega I found myself on the same flight as Fernando Caruncho. I told him that Amancio had spoken to me about him, including the fact that he admired Caruncho's way of life, his extraordinary aesthetic approach. "I suppose," I said, "you did wonders with the house." He replied: "The Anceis house is a delight, and I have a lovely story to tell you about it. When I went to take a look at it, Ortega was very clear about the fact that I wasn't to plan a garden for an 18th century mansion, and that it had to be one that suited the 21st century. I immediately realised that he was dead set against sophistication, and since a house is for its master, not for the person who designs it, I tried to please him as much as I could. We talked about it for a long time before I started on the project, because it's important to get to know your client.

"He looks like a son of the soil; he seems to be looking off into the distance. It's often hard to guess what exactly he is looking at. *He* knows what he's looking at but where he's focusing is a mystery to the rest of us. His thinking doesn't focus on conceptual principles – he seems to be concentrating on ideas that probably emerge from an internal world that he's familiar with and yet are unknown to the rest of us. The surprising thing about this man is that neither money nor success has changed him. He's remarkable, unique among those I've met. And it's exactly this essence he has of being a simple man, a son of the soil as I put it, that makes the fact that he keeps on working, and working so hard, so important. In his shoes I'd imagine that being so world famous would be an enormous handicap. It's very difficult to avoid being dragged onto the 'vanity fair' bandwagon, and he's chosen just the opposite path; he's preserved his privacy as the foundation of his life.

"I planned an agricultural garden project for him. It had the meadows he asked me for, with a big swimming pool for his children, but my ideas went further than he was happy with. 'No one could have designed anything more beautiful,' he said when he saw the plans, 'but I don't intend to do it like that'. I understood what he meant. He was saying 'Don't force me to do this in my own house. I prefer to remain where I am, being who I am, and not claim anything more'. He didn't want an environment where he couldn't be comfortable. It's a serious dilemma: can people actually create themselves, and if so, to what extent? How far can you continue to create yourself without becoming influenced by an environment in which you lose your own personality? These are matters of great importance to him, and he makes great efforts to protect his uniqueness.

"I'm convinced that Amancio is a man with a mission, and the danger of losing that character that makes him stand out from the rest of us could be too great. He is so convinced of what he is and what he has to do that anything that tends to draw him away from that makes him regroup. What he told me was, 'It's a terrible shame that we can't do it the way you've designed it, but it isn't right for me. I prefer to stay where I am'. When you've got enormous strength and a mission, when you're so sure about who you are and what you should be doing, you have no business changing your mind.

"I wasn't disappointed, because the experience led to my knowing this person. We came to understand each other and our friendship grew out of that. It was a very real and sincere outcome. 'What I want to do is to carry on with my own, personal quiet life. Let's call a spade a spade. What you're offering me is something I could never build into my private life, because in a strange way I would be infected by it. For me, it would be a display of greatness, and I want to stay in my place'. I learned something from that, the fact that he didn't want something that didn't fit in with the way he saw his life, however much he liked it."

Fernando Caruncho continues, "Some years passed when I got another call from him. Although my project for the Anceis house had gone nowhere, he showed that he still had faith in me when he asked me to help him with his new house in La Coruña. When I presented my project to him, he said the same thing: 'It's remarkable... but impossible'. The house is lovely, but completely enclosed, with the entrance at the rear. It has a central patio with a skylight. I made him a little garden with a central fountain, and I suggested that he could put a big picture of himself painted by Hernán Cortés on the wall, which is a picture that fascinates him, and frankly, that's the only aspect of my plan that happened. It's a pity he won't take more of a chance. He needs someone to give him a push, to urge him to go for it. That might get me to do great things with him!"

*****

Before my conversation with Amancio closed, I had one more important question to ask. "What do you feel still remains for you to do, after all you've already done? Do you think aside from the huge job of providing work, month after month, for the huge number of people and their families who depend on Inditex, and the frankly millions of people who work for the company indirectly, that there's something else you ought to do that you can pass on for posterity as your magnum opus? Something you want to do for humanity?" He replied saying, "I know that society expects a lot in this vein. It asks you to look at the tragedies, the dangers, the inequalities of the world and it wants you to do something similar to what you've done in the way of business. You're asked to make something. But what is that something? I look around me and see Africa, for example, and I wonder where to begin. I certainly don't want to leave behind a pyramid or a monument. When I look at Africa I see an open door. We've done some good things in Morocco, for example, and in other places where thousands of people have been helped. Of course, it's never enough."

He contrasts this with something closer. Before we say goodbye, Amancio, as a father who worries about the future of his children, talked to me about Marta, his youngest daughter, something he rarely does. "She studied in Switzerland and London. Right now she's in Barcelona, taking care of Bershka. As for the future, who knows? What gives me a great deal of peace of mind is that we've managed to make it to the second generation almost without anybody noticing. I would really hate it if the press decided to make a meal of her. I want her to be left in peace to learn and to work, and then we'll see what can be done tomorrow. The problem of succession is settled, because everything has been delegated."

Taking advantage of this unexpected insight into the family, I ask him about his recent interest in horses. "What made you decide to set up the Casas Novas Equestrian Centre?" He replies, saying, "There were no facilities for the sport in the area, and since I am unable to do things halfway, I think the result has turned out quite well. Now over 200 children can ride. My daughter Marta is very fond of riding and I just thought it would be a good idea to organise some riding competitions, although clearly not just for her. The competitions are in July and September. I just love watching people ride."

9

The Driving Force

"None of us is in this world by accident"

One evening in May after eating in Arteixo, Amancio and I
continued to talk until I had to set off for the airport. It was
that typical relaxed moment we like to make the most of, to get
out of the work rut and tackle more personal questions. On that
particular day Amancio looked radiant and relaxed, quite tanned
from his Camino de Santiago de Compostela pilgrimage.

I told him that the previous summer I had seen the sunset over
Cape Finisterre and how it settled on the endless line of the
horizon. That point (Cape Finisterre) is the very end of the
Santiago pilgrimage that Amancio is so fond of. That evening,
almost night, really, a group of pilgrims were contemplating
this very beautiful spectacle. Nearby was a bonfire where
some of the walkers were burning their boots as a symbol of
leaving behind so many things they had discovered on different
routes through their lives. It all turned to smoke and ashes and
I was very moved by the scene and fell to thinking about how
magnificent the world was. Which led me to say to Amancio,
"And you, with your work, have you made this world a little
better?" It drew him immediately to this passion of his of recent
years that he has talked about at different times. "What we do,
we pilgrims on the Camino de Santiago, is change the way we

see things so that we focus on something that is very important. In a world as materialistic as ours, to live as we do – rather uncertainly just for a while – it changes you for the good. The road leads you to think things out. You find that thinking leads you to find meaning in life, and that's something that you may not be able to do in another environment. By the time you've covered some distance, you find you can't just forget it. I find that all through the year I'm looking forward to going back. When I reach Santiago, after a few days of living in a world that is so different from my usual one, I experience a sensation I find impossible to explain. I almost always ring Flori, my wife, to share it with her. Next year I shall make the journey on the northern road, starting from Santander. And some other time I'll tell you what it means to be a pilgrim for a week."

He continues with real enthusiasm about what those unrepeatable days mean to him, days when he can set aside all those matters that have formed his daily routine for so many years. He told me that he had now made the Camino de Santiago journey four times; twice starting from Roncesvalles and twice from Seville. He was planning to make it a fifth time in 2008 with four of his lifelong friends from the gym. This man who has had the courage, stamina and guts to lead his company, handle its problems and overcome its setbacks, would like to experience a few days that are different, dedicated to something contemplative, something that matters, and that means living like just another pilgrim. Covering many miles a day on foot for spiritual reasons leads to a profound process of self-reflection, supported on all sides by nature.

Hearing him talk so passionately and movingly about the road to Santiago, I ask, having no doubt, "So you're a believer?" He replies, "Yes, I'm a believer. I was brought up in the faith since I was a child and I know that someone or something very important is guiding me. Quite a few years back I underwent a fairly serious operation in the United States. I was scared. At that time of anxiety I made a promise to my 'friend' that if the operation went well I would make the pilgrimage from Roncesvalles to Santiago. I feel bad about asking the Almighty for things. In fact, I couldn't ask for more, after what I've been given. But I place myself in His hands, and He listens to me."

His expression becomes more serious when he remembers out loud that "there was a time when the company was in a complicated situation, undergoing difficulties, and I actually prayed for time. I felt this was my only recourse. It's true, some years back I asked God for some time, because the company needed that time. If I did that now, it would be pure selfishness, because everything is secure. All I hope for now is health and His help to do things well to the end."

This is a valid thought for someone who has it all, but knows that it wasn't just because of his own desserts. He continues to stress the effect the pilgrimage has had on him with a mixture of deep gratitude and perpetual prayers. It helped him to focus his life. The Almighty clearly paid attention to him that time in the United States, because he needed no chemotherapy once his small tumour had been removed. Once this difficult period was in the past, he set to thinking about what the driving force in his life was, "I am absolutely convinced that we're all in the world for a reason. None of us is here by accident. On the pilgrimage I was able to look back and see everything that had happened over the years as an impossible dream. There is a reason for having had an important part to play in everything that occurred. Today it would be a huge undertaking to set up this company, and that's something that makes me happy, but amazed at the same time."

Every word he utters is sincere and I feel his conviction as someone with a full and fruitful life who still needs to be careful not to let his guard down. "The way I look at things nowadays is that I'm aware of what I have, and that reality keeps me at it. Responsibility is the thing that matters. That's what keeps me moving forward." He returns to the subject of our conversation, saying, "I devote six weeks a year to making the pilgrimage. Since doing it for the first time I've realised the extent to which that experience helps me to be myself, to experience humility. I've come to understand how little one needs to live and also, how little each of us matters. But I also got an in depth understanding of what Spain is: a beautiful country to discover in a new way because of seeing it all through different eyes. We cover an average of 16 miles a day, 20 maximum. That means being on your feet six or seven hours a day. During the day we eat only bananas, but in the evening we eat well. My favourite dish, not just on special days, is fried eggs, chips, chorizo sausage and peppers. And it turns out that it's the favourite dish of many people who've come to my home."

I ask him what other things he likes to do on a daily basis: "I enjoy the smallest things. I'm happy with the thousand and one little incidents that happen every day. I go to the gym every morning, I like to chat, listen to people, meet new people, take a stroll, and, of course, work, which is my greatest pleasure. I have the great good fortune of having the kind of personality that doesn't get worked up about anything. Everything has its moment and its reason."

"What about your daily routine? In this little city, do you find you can just lead a normal life, with no upsets?" "Honestly, nobody knows me!" he insists, quite convinced. "Sometimes at the weekend when I'm free, you'll find Flori and me taking a stroll along the Paseo Marítimo. And when the weather's good we head out along the Rías Bajas in a boat I've called the *Valoria*, after the village where my mother was born." And suddenly he's back in the past again, back in the hard times. "What you can't deny is that I always had what I needed. I think the banks understood me because I believed in what I was doing and they thought that I wasn't cheating them. And they were right. Starting with that famous 2,500 pesetas, we've managed to set up eight companies, and there's a new one, Uterqüe, that is launching now. But the most delightful side of everything we've done is that through Inditex, we've managed to change the world a bit. I'm thrilled to find that nowadays businessmen are spoken of in a different way. At least some of us are not just all about money. We have to change that myth. For me, as I've said before, the big responsibility is that a lot of human beings and their families are working with us. I want our business to have a soul. The real success of this company and I insist on this, is the people. I still don't know how it came about, but it's very important, and it's really something of a miracle."

"Pablo Isla is a man who doesn't mind rolling up his sleeves."

Shortly after he joined Inditex, Pablo Isla said to Amancio: "I have to be in closer contact with the warehouses." "It was then that I realised," Amancio tells me, "that he thought the way we did. He's a man who likes to roll up his sleeves and get down to the job, and he really doesn't mind getting his hands dirty."

I cut in to ask what persuaded him to take on this man who was going to turn out to be a key player in the company. (In fact, he has been the president of Inditex since July 2011.) "We ate together, just the two of us, when we were talking about things, and he just came out and said that he really admired the company. He never asked how much he was going to get, just what he had to do. It won me over. I count on people like that, people who don't put money first. There are a lot of really good professionals in that 30-40 age group. In the past you'd bet on a 60-year-old as knowing everything, but not now, they're coming out really mature at 30, because they've had to fight harder. I tell you, this company is a delight!"

The way he talks about it is completely natural, with the pride and concern of the true patriarch. But he doesn't adopt that attitude to boast about his own skills. He says this because he's amazed at the skill of his people. "How could anyone fail to be moved by the thousand and one amazing things I witness every day all around me? For example, I found out Luis, my warehouse manager, had a heart attack right there on the job. They called an ambulance to take him to hospital and there he was, asking for a mobile phone to tell his second-in-command to immediately take over his position and do his job. That's what my people are like."

"Do you really know them all, Amancio?" I ask him. "Remember there are 600 people in design alone," a fact he mentioned with pride and a degree of sadness, because he really couldn't know them all in the same way.

But Ortega feels that he's the kind of boss that the staff are not scared of. "No way. Once upon a time I had an opinion about everything, but not now. When I delegate, I fully accept all the consequences. I found it hard to let go of the commercial side, but I had to do it. Anyway, it's a good thing to give people independence and responsibility, but I also want them to know that they're never on their own. I want them to feel that I'm always there for them, at work as well as in their private lives."

And to bear out his story he mentions the fact that right now he has to make sure he knows what's happening in the life of the journalist responsible for IN, the Inditex house magazine. She has to do a lot of travelling to Barcelona because her mother is ill. He sets her mind at rest. He knows she's a responsible woman, and that right now her top priority is her family.

Beatriz Padín: fresh management at Zara Woman

To get an idea of the extent to which the things I am hearing from Ortega match the reality of what is happening in the company, I have an appointment with Bea Padín, a woman to whom Amancio has delegated one of the key areas: Zara Woman.

The central Inditex building, where the general offices of this huge organisation are located, houses what could well be seen as the heart of the company. It is a huge hall where the designers and marketing staff work almost cheek by jowl. It is a granite, glass and aluminium building, of impressive proportions, collecting and reflecting the often less than brilliant light of this corner of Galicia. The founder of the Inditex empire invested not only a sizeable fistful of euros here with a considerable number of zeros after the digits, but also an incalculable quantity of time, care and attention, not to mention the installation of the wise women who steer its innovative spirit and ensure that its approach is a blend of modern and classic styles.

It is here that you find the office, or rather, the table where every day, since the opening of the building, Amancio Ortega sits in order to get a hands-on feel for everything that happens. One of his main ideas, as he explained in June 2007 to the business school professors with whom he was meeting, was that "you have to boost the unity shared by the design and marketing areas. The product has to be right." Ortega had no hesitation in doubling the area of the design zone, because the balance between the product's quality and its distribution in the shortest possible time is what drives the unstoppable success of his business.

Another floor of the same building contains the pilot shops of the various brands, and within the Zara 'shop' is a huge section called Woman. In other words, all the garments aimed at women, from the high end, Zara Woman, to Basic or Trafaluc, Circular, Punto and Accessories.

That particular day I was on my way back from Milan where I had attended a meeting organised by the European Union dealing with a current and very thought-provoking topic: "Innovation and European fashion in tandem with the values of the European Union. A win-win formula". A number of the speakers from various countries in the Union made references to Zara as an exponent of vertical integration when speaking of the present landscape of this industry. They also saw its business model as very futuristic for the sector. It was easy to see their remarks reflected in what I saw in front of my eyes: the women's clothing pilot shop in its purest, minimalist style; sombre, with wide spaces, good materials and a perfect distribution of product according to colour to make the customer's search easier.

I am welcomed by Bea Padín, a young woman in her forties although she looks younger, perfectly integrated into the environment that surrounds her "domain". Ortega handed her the management of this part of the business, which is effectively 60 per cent of the total company. She's wearing a beautifully cut suit, a white blouse and her hairstyle perfectly matches her personality.

What is most striking about this top chief of the Woman line, the favourite of "Mr Ortega" as she very respectfully refers to him, is the great simplicity with which she speaks and reveals her "work duties" or her huge responsibility, with a blend of unlimited excitement because she loves what she does, and restlessness, "because we can always do better". Yet again, I am a witness to the unmistakable stamp of the house, the brilliant legacy of the man who launched this empire. Bea reassures me that "this has been a continuous lesson I've been learning from Ortega since I started working for him when I was 17." Thanks to the continuous in-house promotion system, Bea now runs one of the star departments of the company.

Her parents were emigrants from Galicia to Switzerland, and when they came back to Galicia, they started a workshop that did a lot of work for Zara. Wondering whether I shall find confirmation of the critical stories which surfaced at one time in the history of the empire, I mention what used to be said about exploitation in the workshops in the early days. Gently but firmly she roundly denies any such thing, pointing out that the workshop paid her parents quite enough to provide their children with a very good education. "The workshop served us all very well." And in actual fact, *this* is the story you will hear again and again in the little workshops of Galicia. "Here, everybody loves Mr Ortega because we live and are who we are thanks to his work and his generosity. I'm not ashamed to tell anybody who wants to listen that I was raised in a clothing workshop, and that my parents worked for that man."

The management of Zara Woman has fallen onto the capable shoulders of Beatriz Padín and she feels nothing but gratitude to Amancio. "I feel thrilled to think that he has entrusted me, 100 per cent, with all the responsibility for this area. I should add, however, that I like to know he's around. He has the ability to observe everything that happens around him; he watches, he comments, and what he says is always worth hearing. He has a quality I have not found in other people that leads him to intuit at any time what is going to be successful. And still, after so many years, day after day, this ability is as strong as ever. I simply have no way of explaining it."

The first thing that Beatriz found herself doing for the business was ironing, on the 4pm-11pm evening shift. One year later she went to work for Ortega, who asked her to transfer to the design and production building where they tested prototypes, and where her opinion on them was needed. Because she loved fashion and was a very normal girl, one who dressed simply not extravagantly, like the many, many thousands dressed by Zara all over the world, she moved over to work on the design team, trying out new models.

It's strange to hear her say that "Mr Ortega has been like a master and father to me. He's caused me more tears than anybody, and I've never stopped loving him. He's very strict, very unconventional. It was years before he told me I'd done very well. When he finds out that someone on the team is capable of giving a great deal, he wants it all."

In tandem with this character reference that sometimes makes him appear merciless, you also find no lack of people who describe him as a "humble man". I'm impressed to see that humility, a virtue so rare today, is the one that is most used to describe the personality of Amancio Ortega. Anybody who has seen him perform his daily rounds will tell you that in this section you only get two minutes of glory: when the pilot store that is the model for the whole world is set up and the first time that Ortega supervises it. From then on, every effort is concentrated on working out which aspects can be improved, which features didn't turn out the way they had hoped and so on. This is another of the legacies that are most pleasing to the president, the fact that nobody can ever say, "we've all done very well, so now we rest on our laurels".

All the departments that depend on Zara Woman are coordinated from this pilot shop. This is where the initial drawing emerges, a sample of which is sent to be turned into a pattern and then a test model that is made in the factory. Once the team is satisfied, it goes out for sale in the shops.

This entire section, and you could almost say the whole company, is at the service of the shop. "It's the customer who's the boss," Bea tells me, using almost the same words as Ortega himself.

New products are kept for a full month in the pilot store before being sent out to the shops. Each new article is photographed and then sent out to each of the Zara stores throughout the world with some general guidelines about placing it. The guidelines mention the essence and the chromatic inspiration, but you have to remember that a shop in Canada will not be the same as one in Mexico. Within the shared character that identifies the shops, each country has its own nuances.

One hundred and seventy-five people are at the orders of Beatriz Padín, all design professionals with their essential staffers who handle merchandising, decide on colours and the internal placement within the shops. The display window, which is unconnected, is a whole art form in and of itself.

When I ask Beatriz where she gets her inspiration, her reply is that she criss-crosses the world with various department heads to keep abreast of what is happening. Everybody contributes their ideas about what they see that is new, and they always operate as a team. This is an infallible rule, another of the features stamped on Ortega's company. "When he was the one doing the travelling, he was able to communicate powerful images of everything that was engraved on his retina, nothing was kept back. And this isn't just a memory of the past," Bea continues. "Ortega is just back from Rome where he went with his wife and some other couples, a trip that had nothing to do with the business, but when he came back he said, 'Bea, I want you to check out what I've seen – leather jackets, a lot of grey sweaters and flannel skirts and trousers'. He's fixated on observing the way women dress and then working out what would be modern and successful, just to keep us up to date. He never fails!"

The Zara customer is a very active international woman, but Amancio wants to sell to everybody. "A lot of customers are asking for larger sizes," says Bea, "and we've tried to meet that demand. But often those items don't sell so well because when people see them on the hangers they feel that the proportions are wrong and that they won't fit. You have to take care of every detail, from the raw material to the finished product, so as not to lose the Zara essence. We're very critical about what we do. If we work with a fabric that doesn't feel right or we don't know what to do with it, we can't feel proud about having sold it."

This is another of the legacies that Ortega has bequeathed to his people. "On every wall and in every corner of this business you'll find the words of advice he's drummed into us, what I call the 'Ten Commandments'," says Bea. She hurries to reassure me that she's not the only one who feels this respect and loyalty for their president and founder. "If it ever happens that he arrives five minutes later than the normal 11 o'clock, which is when he appears in this section, we're immediately wondering what's happened. We miss him, he communicates a kind of special energy that's very hard to define, although the next minute he might be merciless in his demands. There are times when we hate him, yet we still admire and love him. The result is that every single person in this business feels that it belongs to them. It's the only way you can keep going when times are tough."

Bea has been married for 20 years and has a 16-year old son and a 10-year old daughter. She says she has no problems balancing home and work despite the fact that work gets harder by the day, because she has a terrific mother-in-law. "Blessed grandmothers", we both say almost in unison. I ask her if Ortega is aware of the fact that she is fighting on two fronts. "He's always cared for me; in fact he's spoilt me. I never had any problems of that kind. But I have to say I've never had to juggle my time. In fact, when I was first married, he was always saying, 'Go on, have some kids, it's a wonderful experience. Be happy and enjoy them'."

Nowadays Ortega has delegated a large part of the company to others, but as Bea says, with warmth in her voice, "he did it in the most selfish way. First, he carved off what he liked least, and this area, where he's spent so much of his life, was the last to go". You can see that he really has delegated a range of important jobs, but he still stays active in the rearguard for when the most crucial decisions have to be taken.

We take a walk through the plant where the pilot stores and display windows are – they show what will be on the street in a few short months. Suddenly Bea stops to look at the jacket I'm wearing, a special off-white fabric with tucks that give it an original touch. The main thing is that it's comfortable; the kind of jacket I can wear any time of day and that won't wrinkle. She knows that after the interview I shall be meeting Amancio, and laughing, she says, "I'm absolutely certain that tomorrow he'll ask me if I noticed your jacket, because he's done it before". When later Amancio said he liked it, I repeated what Bea had said. Bea had been very firm about the fact that Zara doesn't copy, as some people have suggested, but that they are inspired by what they see. If "world design looks toward Europe, the fact is that almost all our designers are European."

One of the features that Beatriz Padín emphasises in our chat is that at Inditex, "there are no stars. The teams are made up in such a way that it doesn't matter if anybody leaves, the team keeps on working because we have excellent managers in each department, top professionals in every section, and every one of them can keep the work moving forward as if they alone were essential". Yet again, she reiterates the fact of the company's immediate capacity to react or respond which swings into action anytime somebody feels something is not right. "An item can be revised or a product shifted from one store to another, because merchandise that doesn't sell can't just be left. It has to work on the very day it comes in through the door; if not, it's no good. It can't be allowed to take up a single inch of sales area. That's why the collections are so dynamic. And now, with climate change, we are tending to have no proper seasons. Buying is almost on a quarterly basis, which means that section heads have to keep buying raw materials. The top of the range comes from Italy and a lot of the rest from Asia. Decisions are made in Arteixo as to what is needed at any moment and the fabric buyers are the people whose job it is to choose fabric in Shanghai, Hong Kong or India."

As she explains the process to me, I find myself fascinated by the origin of the models that start from Spain, to end up everywhere in the world, the original starting points for the inspiration. Bea tells me that when they visit various countries, a great deal of what they see on the street gives them food for thought as regards colours and trends, but what they really find inspiring is to visit the shops in Paris and New York (if they want to find a basic sweater with the correct length, the right details) or the London shops when they're searching for something on the younger side. It's a fact that when they choose products they can never be certain whether a given collection will be equally well received by customers from different cities.

When Bea pauses, I ask her where she thinks Ortega gets his aesthetic sense from. She says that "since Ortega is a very practical man, he applies logic, not some special feeling. If he notices that a woman is comfortable with a suit and a black sweater, and if she suddenly wants a grey flannel skirt with wide pleats and he thinks it will sell, then he makes it. His secret, as he himself puts it, is to 'use logic to decide and to manage. There's no need to complicate things'."

Bea remembers that when Ortega offered her the position she now holds she was really scared; she thought she would never be able to keep up with him. But he gave her lots of encouragement, and one of the first ideas he was careful to have her take on board was that you must never say, 'I don't like this collection', because everybody plays a part in company projects. 'You always have to speak in the plural. 'We've made a mistake', was what Ortega told her. He would be the first person to say that what we're talking about is our collection and our company. 'So never talk about anything *you've* done, Bea. Say that your team has done it'.

In a sudden rush of enthusiasm, the head of Zara Woman offers me this confession, "Mr Ortega is a very special person. I wish he could be around for another century. He's built up a very healthy sense of competition between brands. Uterqüe, the last one to come onstream, is just the same. Every morning I check the sales of all the companies and then the Zara sales. Obviously I want to see them all selling, but if we can sell a bit more, so much the better. Zara is currently responsible for 65% of sales."

Like a true Galician, she doesn't commit herself when I ask her if she likes present-day fashion. She says that she takes a look at all the catwalks on the internet and she feels that the routine should be broken. "Women have changed. The latest fashion is less and less important and what women want nowadays, above all, is to be well dressed. They want good quality basics. Fashion nowadays has no option but to be practical if it wants to reach everybody."

Before we finish the interview and leave the building where Bea Padín has shown me the new models, I ask her if she would be kind enough to summarise the formulae for good governance that she learned from her boss over a period of more than 20 years. Many are simply brilliant for their straightforward common sense:

- Decisions must be based on logic.
- Be objective with people and always try to put yourself in their place.
- Management is not a qualification. It means teaching, but by example and support.
- If you want to judge something negatively, then you must come up with an alternative.

- Always use the plural when talking about work. Never say: "I did this."
- Concentrate on details. Keep your eyes and ears open.
- Treat suppliers with a great deal of respect.
- We are surrounded by competition. Never underestimate anybody, as very large companies have managed to crash.
- Decisions must be flexible so that the core business doesn't suffer. It can't be allowed to fail.

Of all the pieces of advice that Bea has received from the horse's mouth, there is one that takes precedence over all: nobody is bigger than the company.

10

"There's Good and Bad in Everybody"

Monday 23 June 2008. It is early morning, a few clouds are in the sky in La Coruña, and the temperature is perfect; the harbinger of a typical sunny afternoon on the Galician coast. The day before was the Spain-Italy Euro Cup game that Spain won on a penalty shoot-out. Everybody slept in a bit, because we had all stayed up to watch the match, and Amancio said to Pablo Isla and me over breakfast, "you absolutely had to discuss that triumph and make the most of it. It was great to see the crowds in the streets, just over the moon, proud of the team, proud of being Spanish! When the chips are down, things are really very simple, not like the way we sometimes see them, through the lens of politics. I didn't go to sleep until past two in the morning. And I really couldn't get up when the alarm went off, so I didn't go to the gym this morning."

Interested, I ask Amancio what his usual sleep routine is like, wondering whether he's one of those lucky creatures who hardly need any sleep to be able to work, but he replies, "The fact is that I sleep very well. To function properly, I need at least eight hours."

In the same dining room in Arteixo where we have talked on previous occasions, we start the meal with some fantastic scallops. My host stays with the first course, because, although he's not on a diet, he likes to take care of himself. The atmosphere is easy, relaxed, and Amancio talks about the previous day when he went out with his wife and some friends in the *Valoria*, enjoying a cruise up the Rías Bajas, where he spends a considerable part of the summer. "I was born in the centre of Spain, but I've been here so long now that I couldn't live without the sea," he confesses. "I still end up spending most of my holidays in La Coruña, although every year we get away for a while to see something of the world with friends. This year we're hiring a boat to take a look at Greece, which is one corner of the Mediterranean I love. It always sets me to thinking about the roots of our civilisation. The old part of Athens is extraordinarily beautiful. Once when I was there – we were opening a shop – I was taken to a part of the city where you can get a perfect view of the Acropolis. I was told that Onassis liked to have his breakfast in that particular restaurant so that he could drink in the view of the Parthenon. You just never get tired of it!"

Yet again I try to steer the conversation onto more personal ground, but it's like a spring with the pressure removed, and he returns to his usual response. "I've already told you, I don't have a story. It's difficult to talk about oneself. There's good and bad in us all, and what's really important is what you are, not what people say or think about you. You must realise that if I find it difficult to talk about myself, it's because there are so many others who've given just as much as I have to build this company, so many hours of tireless work. Frankly, they've devoted their lives to it. It's like I told you. We know where we're going, and we're not stopping until we get there."

But I keep trying to get him to talk, and although it isn't easy, we are graced with a few sketches of his career, the career that started that famous day when he was only 13 and heard his mother being told that she couldn't get any more credit.

It is obvious that that event was a turning point in his life. "That story changed me for good. That shopkeeper never knew that he was the cause of what happened later. What a battle it was in the early years! When it came to work in those days, I was just merciless – I worked like a slave and a made everybody else do so, too, and it really wasn't fun. I have to accept that. They were hard times, but the long and the short of it is that the phenomenon that is today's company was born from that."

A new kind of company for a new kind of woman

The memory of his beginnings provokes him to muse, "Society, then or now, puts everything into perspective. In Spain we have experienced great changes, and we've moved from a market with four fashion brands to a company like Zara that has succeeded in making it possible for people to dress well, and not just here, but in 70 countries. Our design section is like the United Nations, with 3,500 people from every nation under the sun working in Arteixo and living in La Coruña! This is a very important fact, because it means culture and wealth.

"I had the great good fortune to find what I was looking for to build the company I had in mind. I think I'm a very creative kind of person, and I recognised the fact that another kind of business model was needed, different from what I saw around me. So we set out on that route with tremendous energy, step by step, for sure, but always in a hurry, always pressing forward. The vertically integrated model we've already talked about was starting to become more common. That was when I was being contacted by a number of *haute couture* houses. Armani was one, and he really was an amazing designer and businessman. Some houses we visited ourselves, others came over to look at our premises."

Conversation drifts to the names of each of the brands involved and I see yet again how deeply involved this president of Inditex is in every detail of the company. He sees everything as his business, and you can see his mark everywhere. It's true what the people who know him say: you can't understand Zara without its founder. And I could stick my neck out and say that it isn't just Zara, but the whole of Inditex that is the sum total of this man's intuition, business vision and complete dedication did to turn his dream into reality.

I turn the conversation to fashion itself. "To what extent are you interested in and familiar with more traditional trends? I mean, do you keep your eye on *haute couture*? Have you personally checked out a collection?" His reply is that he never particularly wanted to get involved in the *haute couture* world, although again he repeats the fact that the most important companies, that is, the top luxury names, certainly talked to him. "But I realised years ago that modern consumers all over the world are actually looking for another type of fashion. For example, we've just opened a shop in Croatia that is doing incredibly well. Women are just mad about our clothes for the simple reason that they can afford them. A few months earlier we opened in Colombia, and it was a real show. I watched the video. People came into the shop clapping and congratulating and thanking us. Our clothes are never extreme – extremes don't sell. What women find is a much more balanced kind of garment. The large majority of women are not in a position to break the bank just to dress themselves. I know some wealthy people, who spend very little on designer clothing. When customers get used to a good quality/price ratio, not just in our stores, but in others at the same level, they feel pleased with themselves. These are people who know the value of money and want to spend it on other things.

"From that point of view, women have become more practical. We all want a nice home; we all want to travel, educate our kids, etc. The important thing is not to throw money away, so that the budget balances. All too often we like to think that the general public doesn't know anything, and we make life complicated for ourselves, when all we have to do is make sure that youngsters learn values so they can tell the difference between what's important and what isn't."

Quite suddenly he's in the past again, thinking about the first years of his life and comparing them with how things are in the modern world. Such a contrast prompts him to say, "Of course, at that time kids were kids, not little adults, and we lived in a village. We entertained ourselves making (archery) bows with umbrellas and throwing stones at each other like idiots. City people know about gang wars but we just played football and nicked pears from orchards. Youngsters nowadays are a different breed. They know so much, they know about principles, respect. They live in the real world. They have the means to be much better qualified, and a lot of them are. It's mostly a pleasure to listen to them, even though some of them are a nuisance with their partying and drinking. Children do have to be taught what is meant by a healthy life."

Uterqüe is born

Uterqüe, the latest Inditex chain, has become another focus of women's interest, this time for accessories. You only have to open your eyes on the street and leaf through a few magazines to see that today, it is accessories that matter.

I ask him the reason behind the name, a Latin word. "The names of the chains have to be just one word, if possible, because they're easier to remember. And it's best if they're short and sound OK in other languages. The problem is that once you've decided on the right word you have to make sure that it hasn't been registered as a trademark. That's sometimes surprisingly complicated.

"As far as the new brand is concerned, I was once out at sea and I saw a boat with a name that had only three letters in it. I thought it was perfect and right away I called Antonio Abril, who handles these matters, to get him to register it immediately. My hurry was wasted. Nothing could be done because it had already been registered. It was Antonio who pretty soon came up with Uterqüe, meaning 'both, each side, each party', and we liked it. Now we have to see if it works!"

I am simply amazed that he's so deeply involved in this company that he looks out for names. I then remember a recent conversation I had with a friend of mine, a financier, who told me about the impression he was left with when he was in Arteixo with two of the company's top managers, a few months before. He said that when Amancio joined the meeting, it was he who did all the talking, settled all the matters on the table, and without really intending to, left the indelible impression that he knew the business inside out and that he was really still guiding it although in theory, he only acts in the background and is surrounded by a formidable managerial team. This friend's perceptions always hit the nail on the head. For example, talking with Ortega about the success of the recent Zara opening in Seoul and the prospect for expansion on that huge continent, he commented, "The Chinese are all businessmen. In actual fact, it's the Chinese who are boosting the economy in Cambodia and Bangladesh, where they're building workshops and factories. The future, and we're watching it happen, is in Asia."

A man with an open mind

Amancio continues to be a man without locked-in opinions. He's a liberal, even slightly leftish, although, as he says, "Nowadays, when I look around me and see what I see, I really wouldn't like to put any kind of label on myself". He's concerned about what is happening in the western world and wonders what the political and social future will be. Ortega, the multimillionaire who created a colossal empire with incomparable business figures, tells me that the shocking inequality that exists among human beings causes him headaches.

"Each one of us has a different part to play in life. Why is mine so different from the person who sweeps the streets or lives in some frightful slum? What could I possibly ask for, on top of what I have? Maybe to have studied for a degree, but I didn't do it because I had other matters to attend to. The great right we all have is to education, because it is education that lets you develop your capacity or the gift you have. I still believe that it is not fair to live in a world in which so many people have no chance of ever reaching a standard of living where they can hope for a better future."

To clarify matters and also to avoid tumbling into the kind of Marxist pitfalls that have misled so many, we move on to the great subject of freedom. "How do you see freedom, Amancio?" I ask, going on to say that, "In my case I think the best example is the family, where we all have the same means, get the same education, live in the same environment with the same possibilities, and where each individual makes his or her own decisions – not those of their brothers and sisters. The justice you seek is in the Gospel, which is revolutionary in the sense of social justice. But what's the formula for making the gift you talk about work?"

Pablo Isla is listening to us, and he interjects with an explanation about what democracy means at the global level. "Despite its obvious shortcomings, it's the best solution for the majority of the highly complex problems that assail us on all sides." Ortega likes Pablo's comment that the most pressing goals are what must be sought first, education and public health for all. He adds that, "In life, the important thing is to strive to do whatever it is you believe you ought to be doing, to be where you believe you should be. From my point of view, Inditex is a concept, not a structure, because fashion emerges from knowledge of the customer, and then serving the customer. For example, any number of things has been suggested to me, even Zara hotel chains, but I turn them down. That's not us."

Ideas can come from anywhere

One question that perpetually turns over in my mind is about the supposed copies in the world of fashion. I mention to Amancio that only recently, someone who works for an Italian luxury group assured me that Zara was faced with lawsuits for having reproduced their models. "I reassured her, as I have defended the company on a number of occasions, saying that what Zara does that no other organisation is capable of, is channel market trends. In your shops you can see garments with Prada, Chanel or Armani styles, but I'd like to hear your opinion." His reply is good-humoured and realistic, even though it is a sensitive area. "Ideas can come from anywhere. I'll tell you something: I actually go out of my way *not* to see the other groups' collections, but I get to know what they are anyway. They can accuse us of being plagiarists if they like, but the truth is that among all the great brands, and the not-so-great ones, there are always areas where they coincide. It might be better to refer to that process of mutual influence as 'inspiration'.

"What gets communicated in a way I find hard to explain is the concept of what you're trying to do, that in my case always arises from what I think the customer is waiting for. If I see something that I think is going to please the people who shop in my stores throughout the world, I adapt it. I don't have to see the catwalks: I see the street, a magazine, something in a movie, etc. and that's what sticks in my mind. One day, for instance, I was in the car stopped at a light, and a scooter pulled up alongside me that was ridden by a young man wearing a denim jacket covered in badges. I liked it; I could see that this was new, genuine, trendy. I called my design chief from the car and told him what I was looking at. In two weeks, the jackets were in the shops and selling like hot cakes. That sort of thing happens to me a lot.

"Another source of inspiration for me has always been the big Paris fairs, like Première Vision, or the Milan fair, although I never go in to look at the stands. What I like about those meetings is seeing people, because people who work in the fashion world are usually dressed in an amusing way, an original way. My head fills with ideas, colours, shapes – things that are different, because of the influence of the opinion shapers who are always in the vanguard. I find I can become imbued with the most forward-looking models. And then again, of course fashion is cyclical, as are colours, and everything comes around again for another season.

"The best advice I can offer to anyone who wants to break new ground is to watch the street. That's the great catwalk. I'm not so interested in the other catwalks. If you were to lock up my friend Armani or any of the other geniuses in a room where they couldn't see out, in two days they'd stop being creative."

I'm delighted to listen to him express the same ideas I've often heard from other great designers such as John Galliano, who told me in an interview that when he was looking for inspiration he would take a stroll through the streets of London, or look around a museum, or he might take a trip to Egypt and immerse himself in the treasures of the culture there before thinking about his *haute couture* collections. Marc Jacobs once told me that his designs were full of memories of Seattle grunge music. The now late genius, Yves Saint-Laurent, in a conversation he shared some years ago confessed that he regretted failing to realise the importance of jeans, because it was the identity symbol of the 20th century. Shortly after, they appeared in his collections with his touch of brilliance.

I have the feeling this particular evening that the president of Inditex is in a trusting mood, so I try to take a peep into his private world, the one he preserves so carefully. My question is, "What is the best thing you see when you scrutinise yourself, Amancio? What's your best aspect?" And to my amazement – I shall never stop learning about this man – he replies without hesitation, "The best thing about me is my goodness. I feel I can say that because it's the goodness of my mother and my grandfather, Antonio. My mother was exceptional. Everybody loved, but *really* loved her! And because I was the baby of the family, of course she loved me, but she thought I was something special. I remember once, before an election, I heard her say 'Who would Choliño – her pet name for me – want us to vote for?' When I started going out with Flori, she once asked her, 'Are you happy with Choliño?' That was the one thing she really wanted for people, she wanted us to be happy."

I interrupt to ask him where the cute nickname his mother had for him came from. "Did it come from the time when you were in the Basque country, I seem to remember they used to call people *'pocholo'* [sweet], and I can imagine *'pocholo'* becoming *'pocholiño'* [sweetie]?" "Yes, that was it," replies Ortega. "And even today, as I told you, my nephews and nieces call me Uncle Cholo. But talking of mother, how clearly I remember her! Thanks to her, I don't have a single bad memory of my childhood. She made me happy. Mothers are the bedrock of a family. When they're no longer there, no matter how old you are, something is broken. Mine died six years ago, and every time I'm in my sister's house, I remember her as though I need to see her.

"At a time like this, when the business is so successful, it's her I miss, because your mother is the person who can add greater value, and truer value, to what you do. Mothers should never die!"

The words of this conqueror, wrapped in the memory of a simple, good woman who transmitted that marvellous legacy of goodness are like a gentle, deep old melody. He speaks slowly and his expression shows no hint of embarrassment when he calls Josefa to mind. I hesitate to break the magic of the moment, but I want him to tell me what the worst aspect of his life has been. Again, there is no hesitation, "The worst thing I can say about my life is that I didn't spend enough time with my family and my children, Sandra, Marcos and Marta. To reassure myself, every time I think I'm not doing the right thing, I say to myself, 'You can't do everything'. But I can't forget my mother's words when I showed up at her house: 'Choliño, why don't you come around a bit more often?'"

My next question is whether he cares about the opinion of others. "It doesn't seem important to me to know how others see me. In fact it never mattered. Anyway, there are thousands of businessmen who've done just the same thing as me. If I differ from them in that I don't spend my life partying or winning prizes, then it's because all my life I always tried to do what pleased me most. I could almost call myself selfish in that sense, since I haven't done just what I had to do, but what I wanted to do."

Before we close, I mention the fact that I would be really grateful if he could suggest how I can encourage the youngsters in my business school who, like so many others, are getting ready with such a sense of excitement for a professional life in the world of fashion. Of course, I realise there are no secret formulae, but prerequisites there certainly are, and Amancio explains them as follows. "The first thing is that you have to like what you're doing, you're passionate about your work. I insist on that because it's very important. It has to be something vocational; you'd almost pay to do it. My thing was creating a fashion, creating a business, creating a chain. Yours is now your school. You know what I'm saying. And along with stamina, there has to be the determination to achieve specific goals. It can't just be about money. That's the way I think. That's the way I am."

We bid each other a fond farewell and he thanks me for the time we've spent together. He laughs because I say that the pleasure is of course mine. He tells me that a driver is waiting to take me to the airport. Indeed, there he is, a young man of around 30, quite a new employee. As we head for the airport, I ask him if he knows Mr Ortega, and he says with a little pride and a little shyness that he's seen him a few times, but he could hardly say he knew him. "So how does he come across to you? What could you tell me about him?" "I don't think he's stuck up. Everybody he meets is greeted and you hear a couple of friendly words. Just think of the power he has, the position he has, and yet he takes everyone into account. He seems to remember his roots. His money hasn't gone to his head."

Nor is he the only person to describe Amancio Ortega like that. They talk about his respect and concern for everyone he comes into contact with.

11

Inditex – The Present and the Future

In my conversations with Amancio Ortega, particularly the most recent ones, we have another regular guest, Pablo Isla. While he has certainly been of enormous help to me in organising both the lunches with the founder and president of Inditex and the interviews with other members of the company, he is of even greater help to Amancio because of his ability to solve practically any problem that arises as though it were the most natural thing in the world.

Pablo Isla joined the group in 2005, thanks to the Korn/Ferry International headhunting organisation and due to the direct instructions of Carlos Espinosa de los Monteros and the indirect orders of Amancio Ortega. Initially he came to work with José María Castellano, who up until then was the CEO and Vice-President of the company. He later rose up in the already vast company. But when Castellano finally left earlier than had been expected, he organised matters so that in less than five months, Pablo was ready to take on complete management of the group as the first Vice-President of the board of directors and CEO.

With a law degree from the Complutense University in Madrid and having become a chief state attorney, he was a very young man at that time. He made the leap from Madrid to Galicia, and more importantly, he moved from Altadis, where he was the chairman of the board of directors and joint-president from July 2000, to Inditex, the Spanish textiles giant. His excellent work with the tobacco company backed by his international experience, knowledge of the share market and willingness to move with his family to La Coruña were more than enough reasons for a group with such a high ranking in the world's lists to take him on.

Pablo Isla's career has been brilliant. From 1992 to 1996 he was director of legal services for the Banco Popular and at the same time, he was appointed general director of state heritage in the Ministry of the Treasury. In 1998 he joined the Banco Popular as general secretary until his appointment to the Altadis group. What connection is there between the worlds of fashion and tobacco? How did Ortega manage to convince him to make such a crucial change in his career and move to Galicia with his wife and children?

To write this book, I made use of all the "lines of investigation" that suggested themselves. The Inditex drivers, who picked me up from the airport whenever I visited were a good source. The 10 kilometre trip to the central building in Arteixo is a nice stretch for picking up clues of human interest, crucial, as our journalism teachers insisted, for getting to know a person in depth and arousing the interest of readers.

I asked one of the drivers, a very discrete man, as indeed were all the ones I met, whether he knew Pablo Isla. His reply was peculiar. To show me how brilliant he thought the recruitment of this particular genius was, he said, "Just think what an extraordinary man Mr Ortega is since he found a Vice-President who won over absolutely everybody the minute he got here! He's straightforward, always has a kind word and always asks about your family or your problems. I see Mr Ortega as a high-power magnet. He only attracts the best and they stick to him."

With this image of a magnet in my head, I sat down for a chat with the Inditex Vice-President and CEO. He was the one who told me that his predecessor, José María Castellano, was very keen from the word go to pass the reins over to him in an efficient manner and make the transition as smooth as possible. Curiosity to know what prompted him to accept such a risky challenge from a personal angle assailed me. I imagined that there must have been something rather special on offer from this company to attract this professional who had so many doors open to him. Without beating about the bush, Isla explained that like most Spaniards, he was a great admirer of Inditex from the point of view of being a customer, as well as due to his business analysis. When it was first put to him that he might like to take over as CEO he found it a very attractive challenge and recognised it as a magnificent opportunity. The combination of a completely innovative business model with a huge international presence and enormous growth potential in an industry as energetic as fashion was a powerful draw. He didn't know Amancio Ortega personally; in fact he hardly knew anything more about him than the official profile.

When I ask him what he thought after his first meeting with Ortega, what impression he went away with, he replied, "My first impression of Amancio Ortega was that I was face-to-face with a man who was a businessman through and through. Here was a man who knew what he wanted, was very sure of what he was doing and what his company meant, and without any doubt, was capable of motivating anyone who got involved in his project. Personally, I took to him immediately. He told me that the decision about who should be CEO was one of the most important in his life and probably the most difficult."

Naturally, I wasn't a witness to that face-to-face, on camera conversation of huge importance for Inditex and for both parties. But by chance, very shortly after that conversation, Amancio himself told me what his Vice-President was now passing on to me, "Amancio didn't ask anything from me." But he said something that in a way, he has always said, 'Pablo, this company is precious. And we have all the tools we need to make sure that it continues to be competitive in the future. Everything is in place. All we have to do is ensure that we don't spoil it, every day'."

After the first interviews he communicated an idea that all his life, as we have seen again and again in the chapters of this book, he has repeated many times, "The most important thing is to see the value in the people who make up this project. You have to love them."

What made an impression on Pablo Isla was something that seemed to be engraved on Amancio's very soul – his limitless passion for the company. That passion is still as strong as ever today, along with his same endless enthusiasm and desire to always do better. "I have to confess," Pablo tells me, "that in the four years that I have worked alongside Amancio Ortega it is almost impossible to love this company and the people who make it up, more than the president. Apart from the fact that he genuinely does, and fiercely too, he transmits that to us all. You become imbued with that attitude, although I have to say again, he's way ahead of us all."

I have to smile because a few days before, when talking with Amancio about taking on Isla, his words were "a blessing from above". He told me that he was delighted with him, and saw him as "one of us". From the first day, Pablo Isla displayed the same lively interest in the new store in Seoul, the best one in Milan, the one in Vittorio Emmanuelle or the amazing shop in Salamanca – a work of art – as in the warehouse or workshop in a small village in Galicia where special garments are finished for one of the factories. Plus he already knew a lot of the staff members by name and was taking an interest in them.

I get Pablo to tell me how he tackled his role as top executive in this company that he already knew and admired from afar. In the down-to-earth fashion with which he approaches life he said that he spent a long time familiarising himself with the financial statements, profit and loss statements and accounts, etc. with a view to becoming familiar with the heart and soul of the company. He added that he wanted to find out just what it was that made the business tick, "because from my point of view, if you don't know that, you have no chance of steering this business into the future. There are two aspects to that secret that are both equally crucial: the product and the shop."

It's illuminating to find out how he learned so much about fashion in such a short period of time. "From the beginning, by observing the real masters we have here in-house, I was working to stay very close to the marketing and production departments by listening and watching."

"So how do you manage nearly four thousand shops?" I ask. "One area that a great deal of effort and energy has to be devoted to is an analysis of the expansion process, because that is where the future lies. This has to be combined with consolidating what has already been built: customer care and the operational system of the shops. This is where you find the heart of Zara as well as of the other chains." In this sense, as attested to by the other interviewees in these pages, the store managers play a very important role. "The shop managers are like general managers, it's a very good position. A big shop is a business in itself. Think about it – some of the shops have over a hundred people on staff."

I ask him about the organisation of the shops from the human resources angle. "In a store there are eight essential players: the boss and the second-in-command in each of the three sections, the central cashier and the person responsible for garment coordination. It's vital that they reach these positions through internal promotion, something that happens in almost a hundred per cent of new openings. There are some countries where this is not possible because of the speed at which the company is growing, but if that happens, a lengthy in-store training period is required. Managers are almost always natives of the country where we open.

"When a shop is opened and set into motion a support group is always in position for a period of time that may be anywhere from between a week and three months, depending on the location and the circumstances affecting the store. Everybody is kept fully informed about what the store needs. For example, an in-house report that covers each opening is drawn up and that report goes to the managers in Europe, Asia or America, to the manager of the chain and to me. It contains first impressions about how sales are developing, an analysis of the way the shops are finished off and whether those eight key figures I mentioned before have been promoted from internal positions or not, what training they've had and what kinds of support teams have been in place."

I find it interesting to check Isla's take on what Amancio has said on other occasions about the types of garments that are sent, depending on the destination city or country. Pablo tells me that, "we don't produce different garments for each city, but there's also no doubt that a shop in Velázquez Street in Madrid is very different from one in a medium-sized city. The changes arise from the orders sent in by each manager that are routed via very advanced IT programmes. It's a combination of intuition, the human factor in customer and market recognition and a rational analysis of the data on the basis of accumulated experience."

On the matter of the appearance of new technologies, the Vice-President is of the opinion that, "like everything we see in our homes, shops have also experienced a communications revolution. Every week store managers receive both a video of the collection plus information about innovations via what we call the Store Management Terminal (SMT). This little computer installed in all the shops that receives all the coordination photographs, descriptions and photographs of each garment so that orders can be placed in light of all those relevant factors."

I tell Isla that it seems strange that in a company like Inditex, all the top management positions are occupied by men. "It depends what you mean by 'top management', since from our angle, the majority of the store managers are women. The Zara Home, Oysho and Uterqüe stores are all headed up by women. We also have women in charge of logistics and human resources, and half the factory managers are women. Apart from the women who manage the stores, the vast majority of the senior staff in the stores are women, and alongside that is the fact that over 80 per cent of the company staff as a whole are women. The store staff are mostly female, as are the people in the marketing and design departments. And there are others."

I talk to Pablo about a rather delicate matter: "Has the company always paid well?" "The philosophy and the aim," he replies, "are to suitably reward efforts made. The plan is to pay better than average for the commercial sector. Inditex does indeed pay well, and there are also sales bonuses to be taken into consideration. But I believe that more important than this is the emphasis we place on in-house promotion, on individual opportunities that exist to grow with the company.

"Anybody who's keen to work, who starts at the age of 20 as a shop assistant, if they like the work and work well, in three or four years can end up as number two or even manager of a shop, an exciting and well-paid job for anybody who likes dealing with customers. They could also hold an important position within the overall company structure.

"In the newer countries we've taken on like Russia or China, where expansion is accelerating, we're working to organise things in the same way. This is something I check on when I visit these expansion areas, whether that means places where we already have shops, or places where we intend to open shops. For example, not long ago we opened a store in the Chinese city of Hangzhou, which has a population in excess of six million people. The manager comes from one of our stores in Shanghai and this new shop is staffed by 35 people. In one of my conversations with the manager, I asked her how many of them she thought would be capable of handling a responsible position when we opened future shops. Her reply was unhesitating and certain, 'All 35'. Obviously, for this to be a reality, you have to motivate the staff to undergo training, and you have to provide resources. It's important for us to be able to communicate our thinking and our culture in each country."

I ask him to clarify what this culture consists of. "It has a great deal to do with entrepreneurial spirit. When someone is given a job to do, they should immediately take responsibility for it and handle it as though it were their own business, whether it relates to a shop, transportation or any other area of the business. This is a culture where you can never feel self-satisfied, one of endless self-criticism. The company philosophy is that you must always improve and do better. We allow a great deal of leeway in management and we are rewarded with good results; the overall balance is very positive. The most characteristic features are a demanding attitude and a lack of conformity."

"Was it Ortega who transmitted this spirit?" I wonder. Pablo's response is, "The company was made by Ortega from top to bottom, in his image and in his likeness. That being the case then, yes, certainly. But at the same time he himself took the steps to make sure it went beyond just him and he did that in top management, at the highest level. I'm not just talking about me here, but other areas that Ortega is particularly fond of: the commercial management of Zara Woman, for example. He's always been familiar with every detail, and has trained a lot of people.

"Nor has he abandoned his involvement, either. You know what he's like – still fantastically active and he has to know that he's organised matters well enough so that today isn't the beginning of a guessing game about what might happen in the future. That's why everybody respects him, well, that and a thousand other reasons. He is very far above average, and the result is that everybody can identify three key factors: his generosity, his huge talent, and his vision for the company.

"The myth of him being some kind of native genius has been dispelled. He is much more than that: he's a brilliant strategist. His passion for architecture and organising space is remarkable, a special gift."

I remind Pablo that, as Amancio is not ashamed to recognise, he has no training. "Maybe he has no academic training, but I can assure you that he has a natural training that is superior to any other from the managerial point of view. He's always alert; he operates far in advance of intuition and common sense. And he has actually educated himself as a result of his natural restlessness."

I try to find out if Pablo sees him as an approachable person, as I have been told by so many who have worked alongside him. "His closeness to people is very impressive: they love him in response to what he's done. It's extraordinary to see how he manages to combine firmness and pressure with respect for everybody, day after day."

I also want to know how he manages to maintain this spirit. Is it enough for him to have become the business benchmark for the 21st century? For the Vice-President of Inditex, "as we've seen, a basic aspect is that the company's identifying marks have never been lost: freshness, entrepreneurial spirit, flexibility and self-criticism. To turn yourself into a benchmark you have to work every day, day after day, as though that day were day one. I agree that we have a sound foundation; we're now present in 80 countries, with seven very strong chains and another new one coming along that we're already very fond of, Uterqüe. We've developed an important logistics investment plan that will allow us to anticipate how the company is going to grow in the next five years, and we are continuing to update this plan on a daily basis. We also have a crystal clear picture of our medium term growth priorities: consolidation in Europe, since it currently represents 80 per cent of our sales, particularly in eastern Europe, Russia, and in the Asia-Pacific. We're involved in highly attractive development of our presence in China, Korea and Japan, as well as in the southern Asian countries. This is because we have become genuinely convinced of the opportunities available in that zone. It's amazing to see how a city like Shanghai can radically change its appearance in a few short months. A lot is happening in that part of the world, they are the real protagonists of this period in history, and a company such as Inditex must play its part in this adventure.

"Lastly, but still an aspect of the values that defined the company, on our road towards the 21st century we have positioned corporate social responsibility and environmental issues as strategic factors that are inseparable from the company. All of our activities whether they be great or small, must express these values. I recall that when we passed the 2007-2010 strategic environmental plan we had been analysing all the important consumption figures: energy reduction formulas, crucial variables affecting the company, etc. I told the environmental manager that we shouldn't just concentrate on the big numbers, but also look at in-house training, including little things like turning off lights when leaving offices and making sure taps were off. I said, 'Just as an example, I would assume the store gift cards would be ecological, but are they?' Well, we had to replace the PVC that the cards were made from with polylactide, an environmentally-friendly biodegradable polymer."

During one of my final conversations with both the president and Vice-President, we talked of some ambitious projects in the pipeline for the development of Inditex in the Asian countries, Russia and the Middle East. I asked Amancio if this would oblige them to sideline their expansion in Europe to some degree. Considering that for a long time I had always accepted that it was Amancio whose hand was on the tiller, I was quite moved when he replied, "We'll be doing whatever Pablo says. It's his decision. Naturally, I'll back him all the way."

By way of farewell, with this declaration still ringing in my ears, I shall repeat the words that I have so often heard from the lips of this brilliant man, "This company is a delight!"

12

Inditex: A Business Model
Pilar Trucios

From the very beginning, with GOA, Amancio Ortega's one obsession was to give the customers what they wanted, and to do it fast enough to meet their demand and at a price attractive enough to increase their purchasing frequency. Until he appeared on the scene, the textile business had taken a completely different course: collections were planned and designed more than a year in advance; products were manufactured during a three-month period and then handed over to the distributors whose job was to deliver them to the shops once or twice during a season. This process involved three crucial risks: an accumulation of large quantities of stock, investment in collections that might have no success in the market and uncompetitive prices due to the margins that burdened every step in the chain.

From the start, Ortega perceived the significant distance between the production process, which was too long and too loose, and the end consumer, the main player on the stage to whom little or no attention was paid. The intention of Inditex's founder was to first put the design and manufacturing together so that the chain could subsequently be completed with distribution and sale in his own shops. This way the customer would become a source of privileged information, rather than just the recipient of merchandise. He was interested in what the customer was asking for and was prepared to adapt the entire production process to satisfy their demands. He was convinced that if he could succeed in completing the cycle, he could reduce his margins by between 70 and 80 per cent, which would have an obvious effect on the sale price for the end consumer. Just by manufacturing according to demand, thus avoiding unnecessary stock, margins would shrink by between 30 and 40 per cent.

The success of Zara, the core of the Inditex business, is based on giving consumers what they want in a sector where it is very difficult to stand out from the competition. What this means in real terms is fashion, continually renewed and at a reasonable price, with a first-rate image in prime locations. This has been supported by communicating ideas such as, "Don't worry; if you made a mistake we'll give you your money back," or "Feel it, try it on, walk around in it, relax," or simply "You're the mistress of the shop". In Zara's attractive environment you can touch everything, listen to pleasant music and be attended by young and fashionable assistants. This is very much the opposite of what had been the norm in traditional chains and stores.

The integrated process defining the Zara business model that is studied by the world's top business schools including Harvard and Stanford, is based on the continuous dynamism of an organisation that revolves around the demands made by the "customer-queen". In the specific case of Zara, the group is able to place a new garment in its shops anywhere in the world within a maximum period of two or three weeks, although this is not the case with the other Inditex chains, as they operate with external suppliers. In any case, with new product lines and the vigorous geographical expansion of recent years, the group has managed to globalise fashion and minimise risk, thereby increasing the size of their target population. The group is unique thanks to its ability to deliver the same collections to stores distributed throughout five continents that have completely disparate cultures. Advertising has had very little to do with this. Zara's main claim is the prime locations of their shops, most of them leased on major streets in large cities.

Although analysts express different views on the question of brand diversification, the ownership of several chains has led to a higher level of stability regarding results. Not putting all your eggs in one basket would seem to be a good strategy.

In the very mature markets, such as Spain and Portugal, it now appears complicated to ask much more of the shops, so growth is currently happening at the international level, specifically via expansion in eastern Europe and the Asia-Pacific region. Spain, with a population of 45 million people and a per capita income of 27,914 euros, has more than 1,300 Inditex shops, while Germany has only 100 shops with its population of 80 million people and a per capita income higher than that in Spain.

The integration process

Design and patterning

The first step in the process is to identify trends. There are three ways in which a garment is conceived:

- The first method operates on a limited scale, and consists of a small office in Barcelona where designers are kept informed of movements in fashion so that they can respond rapidly. Staff members travel from here to as far as Japan or anywhere else in the world, where they note what people are wearing and how the customer in the street is dressed. This can then be converted into designs for the various collections shown in-house at the Arteixo premises. It should be stressed that this takes place on a limited scale as the designers prefer other methods.

- Method number two is to garner information about what customers are interested in by visiting the shops. Designers travel to New York, Paris, London, Milan or Tokyo to immerse themselves in what is trendy in the world's fashion capitals. They observe the dominant lines, colours and materials being used and then take a close look at what is being done with those elements.

- The third form of inspiration arrives in a kind of "everything goes" way via fashion magazines, collections on catwalks, a blouse worn by a TV presenter, a skirt seen at the Hollywood Oscars awards, etc.

A less formal but no less important method of gathering information is also used. This comes directly from the Zara shops themselves, happily supplied by managers who, for example, call in with a comment about a regular customer who has come into the shop wearing something she bought abroad. A powerful information supply connection exists between the shops and head office, although this is backed with more organised systems to help identify the customers' actual requests.

With all the information in their hands, the designers make their outlines and prototypes which they develop with the pattern artists (over 22,000 garments per year). Prototypes are tried out on real people, on dummies, and with nappies included in the case of children's clothes. Once completed, they are shown to colleagues, suppliers and customers. It is common in the Arteixo plant to come across a couple of dozen employees giving their opinions on a collection that some of them have tried on and that the designer is defending by explaining what it is based on and why she or he thinks it will sell.

Garments that pass the test are handed over to the pattern artists who used CAD software to create the patterns. The pattern pieces are placed on the fabric to be used as though they were a jigsaw puzzle, with the aim of making the best possible use of the fabric area. Then the fabric is sent to the factory where it is cut, followed by the making-up stage in external workshops.

When marketing gives its final approval to a garment, quotations are sought from a number of factories regarding costs and deadlines once they have examined the garments in company with the workshops. Whoever comes closest to the estimate gets the work.

Suppliers

If there were just one success that could be attributed to Amancio Ortega from the very beginnings of Zara, it would be his relationship with groups of suppliers who provide him with raw materials in La Coruña. In the early years, on a number of occasions he made the rather slow train trip to Barcelona with his brother Antonio to convince the manufacturers about the project he was developing. The tables have now completely turned, and the Inditex head office receives daily offers by dozens of suppliers prepared to do whatever it takes to work with the textile giant. A large number of countries provide the group with raw materials for producing fabrics and creating the collections.

The Inditex purchasing heads order 65 per cent of their raw materials in advance via Conditel, the company in Barcelona specialising in textiles manufacture that the group owns. They know more or less what will be required – suede, velvet, cotton, etc., and they order bulk supplies in order to avoid stock problems at the start of the campaign. The remaining 35 per cent of raw materials will be ordered once the collection has been decided upon. The production chain ends with fabric dyeing. This is handled by other factories in the group.

Zara entrusts the work on basic garments that don't go out of fashion to their external suppliers. These usually arrive already made up, although Zara's own experts subject them to close examination. If there is one area in which Inditex possesses great competitive advantage it is their negotiating muscle, not just with regard to the shops, but also concerning raw materials and finished garments. This means that a high level of turnover is observed among the suppliers, since requirements are very strict regarding price, quality and speed.

Inditex operates in various ways in the case of garments that are not made in Galicia or the surrounding area. Sometimes the fabric and designs are sent out and the finished garment is collected; in other situations the design and specifications for the garment are sent out to be produced and Inditex can buy the completed item from a supplier, often in Asia, since costs are more competitive there.

Just-in-time production

Once in possession of the pattern and the raw materials, Arteixo factories and external workshops in Galicia and neighbouring countries produce the garments. These are compiled into a catalogue and by using a PDA, store managers can check out what is available and place their orders. If 20,000 units were produced but less were ordered there is no problem. If more are ordered, an operator matches the orders to the existing stocks. If an item is very popular, another production run takes place and another consignment goes out to the stores, although not in every case. If it is a "hazardous" collection, because it has gone out ahead of time or has been affected by weather, for example, the shop is stuck with it. Clothing that is not sold is destroyed after a certain period of time, or according to unofficial sources, is sometimes sent out without the label to small markets in other countries (France and Latin America).

The Arteixo factories, exclusively devoted to "fast fashion" – whatever has to be made right now – are not growing despite the fact that business has trebled in recent years. The main reason is the rise in labour costs. This has led to work being done in neighbouring countries such as Portugal or Morocco. Every day factories send fabric and accompanying trimmings to workshops to be made up as garments. Although the unit cost is higher than in Asia, Inditex can still guarantee "just in time" to supply the whole world. In case distribution to all stores is impossible, then the top 500 receive the goods. Production is organised in line with rates set by the marketing section, which manages all the information incoming from the shops.

The majority of the workshops operate exclusively for Inditex on a very narrow margin. Because of the volume, it works out profitably for the majority. In the last 10 years, especially since the establishment of the corporate social responsibility department, some workshops have closed at the initiative of the group or because they were unable to grow and cope with the cost pressures. In 2003, for example, the Galician group had to shut down 200 of the 1,700 workshops that it worked with because of their failure to meet the standards of the company's code of conduct.

Logistics and distribution

Inditex usually produces 25 per cent of its collection before the opening of the season. This gives it a competitive advantage over the traditional textiles system, since it lowers stock costs and avoids the risk of garments failing to find favour with customers. But this also involves a challenge because it is essential that the distribution to shops works perfectly. Logistics operates at the service of the shops, which self-regulate the flow of products that are supplied from the distribution centres continuously.

Logistics is a fundamental part of the cycle of the Galician group's vertical integration procedure. Stock control in their shops across the world is just as important as fast design and production. This is why Inditex has invested time, effort and a great deal of money in setting up logistics centres equipped with the very latest technology in La Coruña, Zaragoza and Madrid. Inditex also has a returns centre in León, where garments arrive to be withdrawn or sent to other shops. Other chains, which operate slightly differently from the Zara system, have their own logistics centres. The means of transportation most used is by road. Almost everything is carried on lorries except for orders to the USA and Latin America, which go by air. Asian shops are supplied by sea, which adds time to the delivery date.

Shops

The shops are the first and last link in the vertically integrated system, since it is the customer who receives the goods and is the person who dictates what the group produces. The shop manager is in complete control of her territory, be it great or small, with 10 or 120 staff members. Many managers operate as CEOs, and their salaries may be in the area of 240,000 euros, gross. These are the people who place orders from the catalogue and keep the head office informed about what works and what does not. They also organise the shop, although they do this according to foundations already established for all the shops. These foundations are repeated to the last detail, with the same window displays, the same distribution, the same systems, etc.

The shops order from the factories according to their preferences and the merchandise arrives in the shortest time period possible. The stock is held for one month, or two weeks in high season. It is estimated that of each 10 people who come into a shop, three will make a purchase. Inditex has impressed upon the customers the suspicion that what they see on one day will not be there the next, and what is not there today may arrive tomorrow.

Inditex leaves nothing to chance. Everything is established, from the music and the arrangement of the furnishings to the sweets on the counter. Everything is measured according to the shop, the section, the floor, etc. with the aim of maximising the number of assistants available to the customer, since this is the major cost on the profit and loss statement.

Risks and advantages of the system

The main challenge facing this company at the present time is maintaining flexibility while in a period of exponential growth, because it is this that provides it with its distribution capacity and spectacular sales figures. Any shopping centre opened anywhere in the world, regardless of country, provides the best premises for shops in the Inditex group because sales are better. This considerably reduces their costs, thanks to their great negotiating power. They are able to occupy the best shops and even insist on centres being improved.

As Inditex expands geographically and optimises costs, it enjoys significant economies of scale. On top of this, the multi-brand system makes for powerful synergies. Compared with the GAP or H&M, their main competitors, their business model offers a higher degree of vertical integration.

Although the system has been very successful for Inditex, it is not risk-free. Identifying the preferences of the consumer is the key to this model. It is very important to maintain a level of innovation and just-in-time production that has become increasingly demanding in this global economy of increasing labour costs.

Another serious problem that Inditex has managed to sidestep via international expansion is that arising from a presence in a country gripped by conflict. In the majority of these instances they have achieved this by working with other partners, joint ventures or franchises, although once the business is up and running, they usually take over the majority of the companies.

Afterword

"It never occurred to me to write this book." This is the first sentence I wrote on the day I sat down in front of the computer to recount a series of experiences and memories about the unique individual who is Amancio Ortega.

Today, now that I place the final full stop at the end of this work, I find myself repeating the same idea with enormous satisfaction because, despite the endless hurdles I have been forced to jump, I have brought the project home. And as this venture nears its end, I find myself dwelling on one important factor: if it was something more than an intellectual impulse which urged me to write the book, then let it stand that it was the heart, indeed, almost a sense of duty and justice, which would not let me rest until I had gained the consent of the central character. I have been lucky enough to overcome a chain of by no means insignificant obstacles which have lain in wait for me over the period of time it has taken me to set down as much as can be known about this particular businessman!

A large proportion of what is contained in these pages came from Amancio himself in many hours of conversation; and a significant amount, of great value, has come from those who know him and who have helped in the creation of Inditex.

When people ask how great the effort has been and how I managed to succeed, I find myself answering the question the way a Galician would (everything is contagious in life except beauty!) with "it depends how you look at it". It certainly wasn't what you would call easy, to be sure, but at the same time I have to admit that the conquest of this seemingly impregnable fortress has been a driving ambition for me for a good many years. I even think that if I had failed, I should be unequal to making a second attempt – but it's over! I find myself genuinely thrilled by that thought and I hope readers will enjoy reading the book as much as I have enjoyed writing it.

Once the work is out in the world, another entertaining period commences. I shall now find myself obliged to reply, to questions like: "Isn't there anything else in the career of this conqueror?", "Is it possible that everything is as easy as it looks?", "Is that it, then?" "Are you sure you have nothing up your sleeve?". My response to those who have already made this kind of sceptical or critical comment before reading the book is to beg, with all possible sincerity: "If you know of anything, please, let me know, and I'll add it in". And I have also explained to them that if they *did* have any relevant additional information on Ortega, they would certainly have published it themselves, years ago. The fact is that any number of rumours and tales have circulated, all of which evaporated under the glare of reality. The truth is not complicated: this "mystery man" is simply not fond of interviews, and indeed, will defend his privacy tooth and nail, relentlessly, leaving not the slightest crack where his assailants of many years might force an entry, might carry the day in what would appear to the toughest of defences, a defence which I could almost describe as invincible at first sight.

I have been extremely fortunate in being able to spend a good deal of time in conversation with the man, to chat with him on a wide range of topics, and to gain his trust. I was finally able to convince him of the fact that it was important for *him* that the many people who admire him and look up to him (or, indeed, are prejudiced against him, because everything is to be found in this life) should know the truth about him and his career. I said it at the beginning of this book, and I shall never tire of repeating it: there are no words to express my gratitude for the privilege of this approachability and the confidences which have been vouchsafed to me, because they arose as a consequence of the various opportunities I had of chatting with Amancio Ortega.

I should make it very clear that this book is not a biography, nor a lengthy interview. Rather, it is a kind of snapshot in words (he still stoutly refuses to be photographed!), or perhaps a portrait of a genius made up of scattered brushstrokes drawn together by the guiding outline of his day-to-day existence and a fantastic company, designed and developed by a unique individual who, despite what might be expected of someone at his level, remains absolutely simple, approachable and normal. He himself says that he is just one of the team. And in some ways, this is true. But those who know him well reject this, and declare him as one in a million in a thousand different ways – for his intelligence, his capacity for work, his ability to get others to work and his perception of business, but above all they speak of his humanity, his generosity, his humility and the incredulity which is expressed when they see that his success has in no way gone to his head.

I have always liked to believe, and I repeat it here: simplicity is the gift of genius. I should like to think that in some way my book stands as evidence of this.

Should you wish to communicate with me, you may write to me at: covadonga.oshea@gmail.com